A Leadership Perspective for Understanding Police Suicide:
An Analysis Based on the Suicide Attitude Questionnaire

Orlando Ramos

DISSERTATION.COM

Boca Raton

A Leadership Perspective for Understanding Police Suicide:
An Analysis Based on the Suicide Attitude Questionnaire

Copyright © 2007 Orlando Ramos
All rights reserved.

Dissertation.com
Boca Raton, Florida
USA • 2008

ISBN-10: 1-58112-387-6
ISBN-13: 978-1-58112-387-6

A LEADERSHIP PERSPECTIVE FOR UNDERSTANDING POLICE SUICIDE:

AN ANALYSIS BASED ON THE SUICIDE ATTITUDE QUESTIONNAIRE

by

Orlando Ramos

KATHLEEN HENRY, Ph.D., Faculty Mentor and Chair

RUBYE HOWARD BRAYE, Ph.D., Committee Member

DAVID LESTER, Ph.D., Committee Member

Kurt Linberg, Ph.D., Dean, School of Business & Technology

A Dissertation Presented in Partial Fulfillment

Of the Requirements for the Degree

Doctor of Philosophy

Capella University

August 2007

© Orlando Ramos, 2007

Abstract

This study examines suicide perceptions of police officers from two groups, east coast officers and west coast officers. To investigate this problem, the researcher conducted a quantitative analysis utilizing a previously validated instrument. Participants of this study voluntarily completed the Suicide Attitude Questionnaire (SUIATT), administered by the National Police Suicide Foundation. The participants consisted of 75 sworn officers from each group varying in age, education, experience, and job description. This study also examined various leadership styles and makes recommendations for leaders to improve upon or implement police suicide prevention training. Risks factors and warning signs were identified by participating officers, which may assist supervisors in identifying potential officers at risk.

Dedication

This study is dedicated in the memory of New Jersey State Trooper John Oliva, badge #5760. Trooper Oliva will always be remembered as a loyal friend, mentor, and co-worker. The tragedy of his suicide death will never be forgotten.

Your death motivated me to research the subject of police suicide and ultimately completing my PhD. You will always be remembered by how you lived, and not how you died.

Points to ponder

When an officer commits suicide, there are many fingers pulling the trigger.

Leaders are held responsible for those entrusted to their care. These leaders are also accountable to God for those they influence and lead.

Acknowledgments

The completion of this doctoral journey could not be accomplished alone. In fact, many people throughout my life have contributed to this milestone...Thank you.

I would like to thank God for giving the wisdom, courage, patience, and ability to complete this academic achievement. My faith has grown through this process and I pray that this study may potentially save officers lives.

I want to thank my wife Maggie. Although you initially disagreed with the decision to continue my education, you hung in there. I appreciate the additional duties and sacrifices you have made to keep our family functioning during this challenging time. I look forward to the additional time spent with our family now that I am completed. I hope our boys; Nicholas and Evan, grow to appreciate the importance of a formal education.

Thank you to my entire family for all of your support. I want to acknowledge my Mother for her sacrifices as a single parent. You taught me to never give up on my dreams and to always strive to be an honest and respectful man. My older brother Victor, I admire your tireless work ethic and I have always valued our friendship. My younger brother Jayson, I thank you for the quality time we spend together and I cannot wait to present you with your badge when you become a New Jersey State Trooper.

Special thanks go to Mike Harris. You've groomed me from the start. I will never forget the memories and lessons learned as a police explorer.

Thank you to Dr. Alan Arcui and Tony Bethel from the Richard Stockton College of New Jersey. The skills I learned in my first few years of college have prepared me for this journey. Thank you for believing in me.

A special acknowledgment goes to the National Police Suicide Foundation, especially Executive Director Robert Douglas. Thank you for your contribution to the police suicide problem over the past 20 years. You are an inspiration to me and I have enjoyed working together to combat this problem. I look forward to continued contributions together in the future.

To my brothers from Trinity Alliance Church, I enjoy our weekly bible study and thank you for your countless support and prayers.

I want to thank my closest friends: Dee, Adam, Hojo, Juan, Bernie, and Danny. Thanks for great memories countless laughs, and fun times. Thank you to my doctoral friends from the KT. The e-mail and phone support during this process has been priceless. You are a great group of talented scholars, best of luck in becoming the newest experts in your fields. I look forward to celebrating together with our new pillow hats.

To the dedicated educational professionals from my committee, thank you for contributing to the success of my study. Dr. Braye, you motivated me during your presentations at colloquia. I admire your passion for servant leadership and I hope this style of leadership is the answer to the police suicide problem. Dr. Lester, I have to admit I was intimidated to ask you to join my committee. Your expertise in the field of suicide is much appreciated. I admire your extensive list of publications and countless contributions to the field. It was nice to know that you are a real person and very approachable.

Finally, to my mentor and committee chair, Dr. Henry, thank you for putting up with me during this process. I know I can be a little over zealous at times. Your dedication to your learners is commendable. You always returned my e-mails and phone calls in a timely fashion. I will never forget you organizing my initial conference call while I was in Jamaica. We still made it work, Thank you.

TABLE OF CONTENTS

Acknowledgments.. iv

CHAPTER 1. INTRODUCTION... 1

    Introduction to the Problem................................. 1

    Background of the Study..................................... 3

    Statement of the Problem.................................... 4

    Purpose of the Study.. 4

    Rationale... 5

    Research Questions.. 6

    Significance of the Study................................... 6

    Definition of Terms... 8

    Assumptions and Limitations................................ 10

    Nature of the Study....................................... 11

    Organization of the Remainder of the Study................ 12

CHAPTER 2. LITERATURE REVIEW..................................... 14

    Background.. 15

    Discussion.. 17

    Training.. 20

    Leadership.. 23

    Transactional Leadership.................................. 28

    Transformational Leadership............................... 32

    Servant Leadership.. 35

    Research Design... 38

Data Collection Methods	40
Analyzing Data	42
Mixed Methods	44
Triangulation	47
Summary	48
CHAPTER 3. METHODOLOGY	50
Research Design	53
Instrumentation	54
Data Collection	55
Data Analysis	55
Sample	58
Limitations	59
Expected Findings	60
Ethical Considerations	61
CHAPTER 4. RESULTS	63
Data	63
Demographics	64
Findings	67
Hypotheses 1	67
Hypotheses 2	69
Hypotheses 3	73
Hypotheses 4	75
Hypotheses 5	75

    Summary.. 76
CHAPTER 5. DISCUSSION, IMPLICATIONS, AND RECOMMENDATIONS. 79
    Discussion... 79
        Implications....................................... 84
        Background... 86
        Critical Reflection................................ 86
        Organizational Culture............................. 88
        Lens of Autobiographical Experiences............... 90
        Lens of Learner's eye.............................. 91
        Lens of Colleague's Perception..................... 92
        Lens of Theoretical Literature..................... 94
        Recommendations.................................... 97
References.. 100
APPENDIX A. REQUEST TO UTILIZE SUIATT..................... 109
APPENDIX B. APPROVAL TO UTILIZE SUIATT.................... 110
APPENDIX C. DEMOGRAPHIC DATA.............................. 111
APPENDIX D. RESEARCH INSTRUMENT........................... 112
APPENDIX E. LETTER OF REQUEST............................. 123
APPENDIX F. LETTER OF PERMISSION.......................... 125

CHAPTER 1. INTRODUCTION

Introduction to the Problem

Dr. David Satcher, United States Surgeon General and Assistant Secretary for Health published a call to action to prevent suicide in America in 1999 (Satcher, 1999). Suicide was identified as a serious public health problem and noted as the ninth leading cause of death in the United States, claiming 31,000 deaths annually. This was a rate of 85 Americans per day. The same year, the World Health Organization identified suicide as a worldwide problem and urged participating nations to address this growing problem.

The *USA Today* newspaper conducted a study of law enforcement suicides in 1999 and estimated 300 sworn police officers per year committed suicide in America. This suicide rate was two times greater than the rate of officers killed in the line of duty (Loo, 2003). Nearly ten years later, the problem of police suicide has become even worse. According to Robert Douglas (2006), Executive Director of the National Police Suicide Foundation, 447 sworn officers committed suicide in 2005. This is three times the rate of officers currently killed in the line of duty or one officer every 17 hours. Lester (1992) notes police suicides are often under reported and classified as accidents. Police agencies do not have a comprehensive reporting system on completed suicides, suspected suicides, and attempted suicides. There is also a negative stigma, financial motivations with life insurance, and religious reasons why suicides may be classified as accidents. These factors present a dilemma in researching this sensitive topic.

The current literature completed is quantitative in nature. Loo (2003) conducted a meta-analysis of police suicide rates. His study viewed 101 samples of existing literature on police suicide rates. Loo concluded that the rates varied due to the scope of the research. The shorter the time period in the study, the higher the suicide rates. The short time frames and smaller size agencies can increase the mean of police suicides for that year. These quantitative studies show that police suicides do take place frequently. The current research fails to address the questions why officer suicides take place and if there are any training vehicles in place to prevent police suicides from occurring.

Background of the Study

The United States Military is an excellent comparison group to the law enforcement community. Both agencies instill discipline, utilize a unified chain of command, possess stressful occupations, and are considered public servants. United States Air Force (2001) took a proactive approach in developing a suicide awareness program. It was determined that many, if not most suicides are preventable. Since implementing their suicide awareness program, a 37 percent reduction in Air Force suicides was achieved. The Air Force commissioned a suicide prevention integrated project team to research the suicide problem.

It is unconscionable that law enforcement leaders are not following the positive example set by the armed forces, specifically the United States Air Force. The success of the military is an indication that a police suicide awareness model may reduce suicides. The early phases of program development for the Military took understanding the problem. This research is designed to enlighten leaders to the exigency of the suicide problem, evaluate and analyze current law enforcement perceptions on suicide. The information gained may be valuable in creating a suicide awareness model in a law enforcement agency.

Statement of the Problem

The problem is addressing police suicide from a human resources perspective. This study seeks to examine the perceptions of police officers towards suicide. This study additionally seeks to discover information that may assist leaders in identifying risk factors and warning signs in their subordinates that may be a precursor to suicidal ideation.

Purpose of the Study

In order to address the problem of police suicide, leaders much acknowledge that a problem exists and be willing to understand and address it. Currently, less than two percent of the police agencies in America have a formal suicide awareness training program. However, officers are killing themselves at a rate of three times greater than being killed in the line of duty. Recently, California Highway patrol suffered the loss of 14 officers in a 16 month period to suicide. Annually, over 400 American officers a year commit suicide.

The purpose of this study is to measure the perceptions of sworn law enforcement officers, positive or negative related to attitudes toward suicide. The importance of this subject is to address the problems of police suicide from a human resources perspective. Understanding the attitudes toward suicide will enable leaders to better understand the police suicide problem and develop future suicide awareness and suicide prevention training for police officers.

Rationale

The National Police Suicide Foundation recently administered the Suicide Attitude Questionnaire, (SUIATT) to various police departments across the country. This research intends to utilize the raw data collected from the foundation to compare and contrast two groups. The two groups consist of an agency from the west coast and an agency from the east coast.

The benefit of using this previously collected data is the data comes from a reputable source, it is cost effective, time efficient and manageable. It would not be feasible for the researcher to travel across the country and collect data on this large of a scale.

Research Questions

The research questions for this study are as follows:

1. Is there a difference in suicide perceptions based on geographical locations, specifically west coast compared to east coast?

2. Is there a difference in suicide perceptions among demographic categories such as gender, time of service, rank, and job description?

3. What circumstances are more likely to make an officer consider suicide or not consider suicide as an option?

4. Is there a difference in suicide prevention training based on geographical locations?

5. Is there a need to improve upon suicide prevention training?

Significance of the Study

This research is significant for many reasons. First, the profession of law enforcement is known to be very stressful and sometimes dangerous profession. Officers receive formal training in a military style environment to prepare them for the rigors of the profession. This formal training includes proficient use of firearms, self defense, physical fitness training, conflict resolution, and basic police tactics. All of these subjects have one common theme, officer survival. Officers are trained in the academy that their safety is primary and their goal is to go home at the end of their shift.

This research seeks to address a gap in the officer survival training curriculum. According to the National Police Suicide Foundation, less than two percent of American law enforcement agencies have a formal police suicide awareness training program (Douglas, 2006). Resources are keenly focused on training officers to survive armed encounters and dangerous suspects. The reality is American officers kill themselves at a rate of three times higher than officers who are killed in the line of duty annually.

This research seeks to significantly address this problem from two areas, leadership and training. By understanding the perception of officers toward suicide, formal training can be improved and implemented. Discovering additional risk factors, warning signs, and indicators identified by this research may be a valuable resource to law enforcement leaders, and may potentially save lives.

Definition of Terms

Attempted Suicide: Refers to an unsuccessful attempt to end a human life using unspecified methods (Douglas, 2006).

Calls for service: Is defined by the day to day events officers are exposed to which can range from low risk community contacts to high risk car stops and dangerous situations.

Completed Suicide: Refers to a successful attempt to end a human life using unspecified methods. This term is synonymous with committing and committed suicides.

Critical incidents: Refers to stressful and traumatic events that provoke a emotional, physical or stress related response (Violanti, 1996).

Depression: Refers to sadden, sullen mood, or lower feeling state of mind that can affect a person physically, psychologically and emotionally (Thrasher, 2001).

Occupational Stress: Refers to internal and external factors, pressures and burdens as a result of handling calls for service, adjusting to the organizational culture, and interacting with supervisors and administrators (Violanti, 1995).

Organizational Culture: Is the personality of the organization. Culture is made up of the assumptions, values, norms, and identifiable signs of organization members, their behaviors and attitudes (Caldero & Crank, 2004).

Psychological Autopsy: Is defined as a post investigation of a suicide which includes the review of personal and medical records, and interviewing of co-workers and family members to determine factors leading to the suicide (Sewell, 2001).

Risk Factors: Professional and personal life events that can cause elevated stress and or depression (Douglas, 2006).

SUIATT: Is an acronym for Suicide Attitude Questionnaire (Diekstra & Kerkhof, 1988).

Suicide Awareness Training: Refers to a formal suicide training program which educates on prevention, risk factors, and warning signs (Douglas, 2006).

Suicidal Ideation: The fascination and preoccupied thought of attempting suicide (Douglas, 2006).

Sworn Officer: This term represents a full time member of a police agency and is not specific in jurisdiction, such as municipal, county, state or federal law enforcement. The terms Police Officer, Officer, Law Enforcement Professional are used to add variety and are not used to distinguish professional differences.

Warning signs: Identifiable changes in personal and professional behavior which may be an indicator of elevated stress and or depression.

Assumptions and Limitations

It is the researcher's assumptions that the participants in this study may be guarded in their responses due to the strong organizational culture of the police community. As a result of formal training and exposure to highly stressful situations, the participants may minimize their feelings and justify them as part of the job.

There may be differences in suicide perceptions based on experience, education, and time of service. Religion may also be a contributing factor to the officer's perception on suicide in general.

Limitations to this study include the methodology. Although quantitative methods can be more statistically significant and have greater reliability than qualitative, the information can be restrictive. Qualitative research delves deeper into understanding relationships and correlations between variables. Qualitative results may show that a relationship exists but does not qualify why it exists. The subject matter is very sensitive in nature. Officers may be reluctant and suspicious to answer honestly in fear of negative repercussions from their respective organizations.

Existing data on officer suicides is another limitation to this study. Currently there are no local, state or federal requirements that accurately memorialize officer suicides or demand agencies to report them. This discrepancy is noted in the difference in documented suicides by the Federal Uniform Crime Reports as compared to validated officer suicides recorded by the National Police Suicide Foundation.

Nature of the Study

This research entails the analysis of voluntary responses from participants completing the SUIATT instrument. The participants include sworn members of the law enforcement community which consist of various ranks, job descriptions, seniority, and experience.

The instruments do not have any personal identifiable information on them in order to preserve anonymity of participants. The data was collected by the Executive Director of the National Police Suicide Foundation, Robert Douglas Jr. Director Douglas has granted written permission to this researcher to utilize the data collected in this study.

Organization of the Remainder of the Study

This chapter identifies the problem of police suicide and provides a background of the topic. An overview of this research project was provided as well as the significance, purpose, and rationale for this project. Operational definitions were listed; assumptions and limitations for this study were examined.

The remaining chapters of this study include a comprehensive literature review in the second chapter. This includes previous works published by experts and active researchers in the field. Chapter three outlines a detailed plan to carry out the research. This chapter includes the methodology, research questions, population, design of the study, instrumentation, and expectations of this study. Chapter four is dedicated to the results and analysis of the data. The final chapter of this research discusses the conclusions, recommendations for future research, limitations, and summary.

CHAPTER 2. LITERATURE REVIEW

The problem of police suicide appears to be a very sensitive and complicated topic to research. The experts researching this topic do not seem to agree on the frequency and severity of police suicides. Hem, Berg, and Ekeberg (2001) noted varied police suicide rates ranging from 5.8 suicides per 100,000 through 203.7 per 100,000. The bulk of the literature tries to compare the general public suicide rate of 12 per 100,000 to the undetermined rate of police officers. Arguments have been raised that the police suicide rate should be compared to white males in the general public; most officers completing suicides are white males (Loo, 2003).

Although the experts do not agree if the suicide rate is higher or lower than the general public, it is alarming that police officers are eight times more likely to commit suicide than become a victim of an on duty homicide (Violanti, 1996). The police are more dangerous to themselves than the suspects they arrest. In 2005, 447 sworn police officers committed suicide (Douglas, 2006).

This literature review will examine and evaluate the problems of police suicide. Police suicide is examined from a human resources approach with respect to leadership and training to determine the effectiveness of each upon this problem. Recommendations are made to increase awareness, standardize training, and empower leaders in creating organizational change.

Background

Research on police suicide is not an entirely new topic. It has received great attention because the rates are climbing annually in the general population and among the police community. During a six-year period of 1934 to 1940, New York City police suffered the loss of 93 officers to suicide. This rate was twice the rate of the previous six years (Heiman, 1977).

The 1999 call to action by the United States Surgeon General shifted focus to the topic of suicide nationally. During this period the general public was completing suicide at a rate of 31,000 Americans annually. The World Health Organization classified suicide as a public health problem in America and globally. The surgeon general developed and implemented a National Strategy for Suicide Prevention (Satcher, 1999). In response to this call to action all branches of the United States Military implemented a suicide awareness and prevention program, (United States Air Force, 2001, United States Army, 1988). Ironically, law enforcement agencies did not follow the lead of the military. Currently, less than two percent of law enforcement agencies in the country have a suicide awareness program (Douglas, 2006).

Agencies are learning through costly mistakes of ignoring the problem of police suicide. A 1982 case initiated by a wife of a New York City Police Officer settled for half a million dollars. In this case, Bonsignore versus The City of New York, an officer shot his wife before killing himself (Schuckler, 2001). This is a salient case for the police suicide problem because it proved the police agency is not immune to civil liability in the event of off duty actions by a member.

If saving fellow officers' lives does not motivate agencies, maybe they can be motivated by addressing the suicide problem to save the organization money. If families determine officers kill themselves as a result of stress associated with the police profession, and the agency provided no training, this could lead to additional and even more expensive wrongful death lawsuits. Either way police suicide in America has reached levels of an epidemic and need to be addressed regardless of the agencies' motivations (Douglas, 2006).

Discussion

The profession of law enforcement attracts physically fit, educated, and motivated individuals. In order to become a member of the law enforcement community an applicant must complete a comprehensive application process, graduate from a military style police academy, and be approved to ride alone by a field training officer (Violanti, 1997). Members of the police community are subjected to a ridged and structured life style, wear uniforms, and report through an established chain of command (Hem et al., 2001). Officers quickly are conditioned to assimilate into their police role, through observation of peers, interaction with the community, and personal identity, (Violanti).

The idealistic police role that rookie officers so greatly strive to achieve could be the very factor that leads to their own demise. The role of a police officer is a difficult one that encompasses many types of stress, (Violanti, 1996). Police Officer's stress comes from multiple directions, community, managers, administrators, and family. Officers rely on the role of a police officer as a defense mechanism for physical and emotional survival. Unfortunately, officers cannot see that the role is not functional 24 hours a day and is unhealthy in dealing with personal rather than professional settings (Schmuckler, 2001).

Officers are constantly exposed to the negativity society has to offer. Over time this constant exposure to critical incidents, death, frustration, and high levels of stress eventually takes a toll physically and mentally. As identification with this coveted role grows, the officer becomes more isolated from family and friends. Young officers become addicted to the rush of adrenaline faced in daily work related scenarios. Life outside of the uniform becomes less interesting and boring sometimes. Officers feel they cannot relate to others who are not police officers, and they lose trust in anyone who is not a cop (Violanti, 1996).

The role identification of an officer has a snowball effect. The more time an officer has in the profession, the more cynical, isolated, and defensive they become.

These characteristics create an adversarial relationship and are the stimulus of an "Us-versus-them" mentality. Soon an officer's social circle becomes narrowly filled with mostly other officers. The investment in the police role is a 24-hour obligation. Officers are required to carry a firearm and police identification off duty. The identification of the police role takes precedent over other roles such as parent, spouse, sibling, and friend (Heinsen, Kinzel, & Ramsay, 2001).

Understanding the importance the police role plays in officer suicide is critical for leadership and training. Officers on duty feel a need to be constantly in control. Officers take control of their emotions, actions, dangerous situations, and become the consummate problem solvers. A career filled with solving others' problems leaves an officer hopeless when they feel they cannot resolve their own. Officers resort to solving problems in a manner they have become accustomed to, as a cop. When the problems are not resolved, officers feel a sense of loss of control. Loss of control creates anger, frustration, and depression for police officers. Loss of a loved one, loss of their control in their profession and loss of their police identity can lead to the loss of their life (Violanti, 1997).

Suicide has been identified as a permanent solution to a temporary problem. Usually a person is so upset that they feel suicide is the only way to stop the pain and the sense of hopelessness, loneliness, helplessness, and isolation. Research on attempted suicide has found that these feelings are temporary and the pain lessens as time goes on. In order to assist officers in dealing with the difficulties of their profession, they need to be aware of the potential for suicidal ideation. Suicide awareness and prevention can be accomplished through training and leadership (Thrasher, 2001).

Training

Police officers receive roughly six months of formal training in the police academy. This training has an underlying theme of officer survival. The officers are educated in self-defense, physical fitness, firearms training, impact weapons, and pepper spray. All of these subjects are designed to keep an officer alive. Surprisingly, very few agencies teach their officers about the mental demands of the profession, the physical and psychological implications of stress, and the dangers of suicide (Schmuckler, 2001).

The literature demonstrates the success of suicide awareness programs. The United States Air Force reduced suicides by 37 percent after implementing a suicide awareness training program (United States Air Force, 2001). The Maryland State Police suffered multiple suicides in a five-year period. However, since adopting a suicide awareness program they have gone five years without any additional suicide victims (Douglas, 2006). A myth of suicide training is that the attendee will receive the thought of attempting suicide from attending the training. Officers throughout their career have already been exposed to suicide attempts and completed suicides.

The Federal Bureau of Investigation has adopted a holistic suicide awareness program. The FBI recommends training police officers, their spouses, supervisors, and administrators. The program also includes adopting a community policing philosophy to minimize officer isolation. Officers should be encouraged to participate in activities outside of the police agency. Training should include identification of resources available inside and outside of the police agency (Thrasher, 2001).

The focus of the training should include recognizing risk factors, identification of warning sings, and positive coping mechanisms. Stress reduction techniques can supplement physical fitness training and promote an overall wellness. The training can be designed to identify the needs of different levels. In the police academy, new officers should be made aware of the impact their role can have on personal relationships, the community, and themselves (Schmuckler, 2001). Mid-level management can build on the recruit training and learn how to identify danger signs of suicide and be well versed on available resources. Administrators and command staff need to be trained on handling of high-risk officers, funeral protocols, and dealing with survivors of suicide (Sewell, 2001).

Through training, officers can learn to reduce stress in their life and recognize dangerous conditions in themselves and co-workers. There are several suicide prevention models available. A model that has been nationally recognized is QPR. QPR stands for question, persuade, and refer. This prevention program is known as the CPR for officer suicide. The premise behind the QPR program is to be your brother's keeper. Officers through training must me comfortable with using department resources and not fearing organizational retribution from the administration (Douglas, 2006).

Leadership

According to Sewell (2001), management sets the tone for the agency in response to the suicide problem. Management must empower employees to seek help for stress experienced in their professional and personal lives. Many surveys conducted on police stress identified the administration as their greatest source of stress. Leaders must realize that the previously effective command and control style is not effective all the time. This leadership style may complicate the work environment and create a sense of distrust between administrators and members, possibly contributing to increasing stressors. Leaders may want to formally put their plans in place through effective policy creation.

Policy is an effective way of codifying an administrator's intentions and systematically following through the actions now and in the future. Policy with regard to suicide prevention can be effective in implementing and sustaining a suicide awareness training program. Administrators can be excellent resources in setting the example that the organization values its members and their mental and physical wellbeing (Sewell, 2001).

Policy changes need to be implemented with regard to reporting suicides. There is a national database for line of duty deaths for police officers. Currently, there is no systematic way of documenting officer suicides across the country (Hem et al., 2001). There are four acceptable classifications for death in the United States: (a) natural; (b) accidental; (c) suicide; and (d) homicide. Violanti (1995) explains that it is difficult to determine the true number of suicides because many can be listed as accidents. Misclassification occurs to protect the officer from the stigma of suicide, protect the family, and protect the agency from legal ramifications. Administrators must make it clear that misclassification of suicides is not tolerated and those who file false reports will be disciplined.

Leaders can also take a proactive approach in the mental health of their employees. Policy can be created to make employee assistance programs mandatory for exposure to critical incidents. Agencies use these services primarily for officers involved in shootings. Officers may need to see a counselor for prolonged life saving efforts, exposure to a scene of death, sexual assault cases, disaster scenes, and other highly stressful situations (Thrasher, 2001). Literature shows that the previous method of suppressing or compressing the emotional feelings associated with exposure to critical incidents is detrimental to officers over extended periods of time. Creating trained peer support groups, critical incident response teams, as well as providing outside counseling would be beneficial to the mental health of police officers.

The leaders of the organization at all levels must support training. It would be difficult to implement a successful training curriculum if the line members knew that the program was not fully backed by the leadership. In the event a suicide occurs a psychological autopsy should be conducted to determine the factors behind the completed suicide. The information gathered in the post investigation of the suicide could be instrumental in adjusting future training, identifying additional risk factors, and warning signs (Sewell, 2001).

Leaders must take the time to know their people. By understanding the people who work for you, a leader could be the first line of defense when symptoms arise from stress. A leader can prevent the heightened stress from leading to depression by offering support, defusing the stressor, or making a referral to a mental health professional (Schmuckler, 2001). In addition to knowing your members, a leader must know the high-risk high stress units and be cognizant of the level of morale in those units. High-risk units such as tactical entry teams, fugitive units, canine patrols, and other high stress specialties are exposed to critical incidents more frequently than patrol officers.

Coordination with other entities within the organization can be helpful to prevent suicides in high-risk groups like retired officers and officers pending investigation. Retired officers are ten times more likely to complete suicide than active officers (Douglas, 2006). Officers under investigation need to be counseled during this stressful time and a decision needs to be made on the availability of their weapon. The weapon of choice among suicidal officers has been their own duty weapon.

Leaders can encourage positive relationships with the family members of police officers by hosting formal activities. Award nights, promotional ceremonies, and organized sporting events can provide an outlet for officers, and an opportunity to include loved ones in the police family (Thrasher, 2001). Training for family members on the symptoms of stress, post traumatic dress disorder, and warning signs of burnout can help a family member recognize early warning signs of suicide (United States Air Force, 2001).

The literature speaks for itself on the severity and frequency of the police suicide problem. Law enforcement suicides have been researched since the 1930's. It is unacceptable and unconscionable that seventy years later less than two percent of police agencies in America acknowledge the problem of police suicide.

Training officers on the effects of role identification, potential warning signs, risk factors, and life events that lead to suicidal tendencies is a starting point. The law enforcement community should follow the militaries lead and make the training mandatory for all service members, support staff, and critical incidents. The inclusion of family members would be a valuable addition to expand the scope of understanding and protection.

Leadership is an integral component in the success of a suicide awareness program. Leaders need to be liaisons between the entrance process, academy training, and assimilation into the police culture. They must convey their intent throughout the organization and effectively shift the organizational culture into asking for help, assisting officers in need, embracing training, and reducing the stigmas associated with mental health professionals (Sewell,2001). Not all leadership styles are conducive to facilitating a police suicide awareness program.

Transactional Leadership

The primary leadership style in law enforcement agencies is a quasi military, command and control form of transactional leadership (Bennett & Hess, 1996). Bass (1997) defined transactional leadership as an exchange between leaders and followers through the use of rewards, punishment, and formal authority to gain compliance from followers. Leaders under a transactional style of leadership exhibit four types of behavior: (a) contingent reward; (b) passive management by exception; (c) active management by exception; and (d) laissez-fair leadership.

Bass (1997) provided details for each of the four types of leadership characteristics under transactional leadership. Contingent rewards are used to influence behavior. The leader identifies work needed to be completed and rewards members when expectations are met. When employees deviate from standards, the passive management by exception style is used. To produce desired results the leader uses a form of correction or punishment. Active management by exception is an active monitoring done by the leader. Corrective measures are used to meet standards. A hands-off approach to transactional leadership is considered laissez-faire leadership. The leader in this case is indifferent and does not directly respond to problems or personally monitor behavior.

The assumptions of transactional leadership indicate members are motivated by reward and punishment. A clear chain of command makes social systems work best under this style. In exchange for salary and benefits, members submit authority to their managers. The final assumption of transactional leadership is that subordinates purpose is to do what managers direct them to do (Bass, 1997).

Transactional leaders accept the organization's culture, belief systems, and norms. Transactional leaders supply roles for followers through clarification of assignments and motivate members with rewards. Goals are set for members by transactional leaders. Inexperienced members are shown how to perform tasks and are encouraged to continue positive behavior. Experienced members are held to a higher standard and are often corrected or disciplined when they do something wrong (Bensimon, 1989).

Follower's expectations are to be shown how to succeed in an organization and are provided opportunities to improve personal performance. Subordinates are fully responsible for tasks given from their leaders. Despite the availability of resources, skill level, or capability to complete the task, if things go wrong, subordinates are considered fully responsible and may be punished for their failure. In a transactional leadership system, a subordinate's success is contingent upon their performance and the ability to satisfy the leader.

The benefits of transactional leadership include clear cut goals and roles established for subordinates. There is a structured chain of command which is effective in tactical and emergent situations. Desire, commitment, and loyalty from followers can be quickly evaluated through observation and performance. Transactional leadership is a beneficial short term leadership style (Bass, 1997). Kanungo (2001) cautioned transactional leaders to be cognizant of their motives. Transactional leaders use power and positions to obtain a desired result from followers. This style of leadership can be considered unethical if the leader is satisfying their own personal interests, and if subordinates are led to perform in an unethical manner to achieve an end. A common flaw in transactional leadership is creating and supporting an environment where the ends justify the means in order to accomplish the overall mission. Transactional leaders can also become preoccupied by power, perks, and politics. This style of leadership limits the growth, communication ability, and creativity of followers. Transactional leadership has been identified through literature as less effective than transformational leadership.

Transformational Leadership

Druker (1993) noted management is doing things right and leadership is doing the right things. This appears to be the significant difference between transactional and transformational leadership. A transactional leader's role has many characteristics of a manager. Transformational leadership is oriented towards long term goals, creating change, empowering employees, and encourages personal growth for both the leader and subordinates (Bass, 1997).

Burns (1978) identified transformational leadership as an exchange between members that creates a higher level of motivation and morality for both leaders and followers. Bass (1997) identified four characteristics of transformational leaders: (a) a form of charismatic leadership or idealized influence; (b) inspirational leadership or motivation; (c) intellectual stimulation; and (d) individualized consideration. Transformational leadership encourages positive relationships between leaders and followers which increases the willingness to exert effort by both, and creates improved performance and job satisfaction.

Bass (1990) identified three assumptions of transformational leaders: (a) people will follow those who inspire them; (b) a leader with vision and passion achieves great things; and (c) tasks are accomplished through enthusiasm and energy. Transformational leadership begins when a leader shares their vision about the organizations future and the role its members play in it. This style of leadership creates a partnership with subordinates as they take ownership toward organizational goals.

Transformational leaders view their role as having a strong purpose in life, maintaining excellent interpersonal control, and display a calm sense of self-confidence (Sosik & Megerian, 1999). Transformational leaders identify skills and motives in followers and seek to help them grow personally and professionally. Subordinate growth occurs through the assignment of meaningful and professionally challenging assignments that help members realize their potential (Bass, 1990). Overall success of the organization and its members is of greater importance than the personal gains of a transformational leader. The roles of a transformational leader include teaching, mentoring, leading by moral example, and coaching (Benisom, 1989).

The role of followers under a transformational leader is to accept change and embrace the transformation. Followers are encouraged to communicate their vision and identify problems in their work areas. The transformational leader provides the tools for subordinates to succeed. It is contingent upon the member to carry out tasks as trained, and use the tools provided to accomplish the mission. Ultimately, the subordinate through this transformation will perform beyond normal expectations and elevate in the organization (Bass, 1997).

According to Bass (1990), the benefit of transformational leadership is an improved leader follower relationship. Transformational leadership is essential in organizations needing and seeking change. The needs of followers are better met under transformational leadership as both leaders and followers are striving towards a common goal. The litmus test for the success of transformational leadership is determinant upon whether the level of morality in human conduct is raised, as well as aspiration of higher ethical standards by leaders and followers (Burns, 1978).

Burns (1978) indicated that transformational leaders could incur some resistance from members who do not embrace change or feel change is not necessary. Although transformational leaders are filled with vision and passion, others may not fully buy into their goals. In order for transformational change to occur it is a voluntary change from members who also believe in the vision shared by their leader. The leader may be very determined and passionate about their goals and vision, but they may also be very wrong in the direction they are headed. A criticism of transformational leadership is that it is a soft style of leadership where a leader focuses on the big picture and often forgets the small details in between, resulting in failure. Transformational leaders can become very frustrated if they feel a need to lead change and the change is either not needed or members are content with the way things are (Bass, 1990). Servant leadership is a form of transformational leadership.

Servant Leadership

Robert Greenleaf (1977) developed the theory of servant leadership. Servant leadership is service oriented and greatly differs from a traditional command and control leadership approach practiced by transactional leaders. Servant leadership is a practical leadership philosophy which focuses on service oriented characteristics that identify a servant leader. The ultimate goal of servant leadership is to develop your members so they can be successful and a valuable resource to your organization, and ultimately becoming servant leaders themselves.

The three assumptions of servant leadership are: (a) the leader has responsibility for the followers; (b) leaders have a responsibility towards society and those who are disadvantaged and; (c) people who want to help others best do so by leading them. Servant leadership has a two fold criteria, the people served grow as individuals and leadership benefits society as a whole and the disadvantaged (Spears, 1998).

Servant leadership takes a holistic approach to leadership. Servant leaders believe they should provide skills to employees that make them succeed on and off the job. An employee's personal life undoubtedly affects their professional life. Servant leaders strive to be known as leaders who care about family values, community involvement, and nurturing of personal and professional relationships. The focus of this leadership style is people not power. Rowe (2003) identified five virtues of a humane leader; respect, magnanimity, truthfulness, commitment to goals, and generosity. Rowe also quoted Confucius, in support of servant leadership, "Put service first and your own gains after."

A servant leadership continuum consists of characteristics and concepts that define a servant leader. The definition has been broadened over time and the interpretation of its logical flow has been tailored to fit different organizational venues. Larry Spears, President and CEO of the Green Leaf Center for Servant Leadership extracted ten main characteristics from Greenleaf's original writings. The ten characteristics included listening, empathy, healing, awareness, persuasion, conceptualization, foresight, stewardship, commitment, and building community (Spears, 1998).

Patterson (2003) provided variables he felt were supportive of servant leadership from a cognitive perspective. These traits included humility, altruism, vision, trust, empowerment, and service. The variables were expanded again in the theme of social cognition and focused on an individual's thoughts and actions. This interpretation was more application based (Winston, 2005).

Although the literature addresses leadership and training individually, they are very much intertwined. Training cannot be successful if not entirely supported from leadership. Leadership alone will not be effective enough in reducing suicide without creating a shift in role identification, positive coping mechanisms, and training all levels of the organization. Law enforcement professionals represent the brightest and fittest our communities have to offer. In addition to training officers to survive the dangers of police work, officers need the proper tools to protect themselves from the most dangerous suspect of all, themselves. Servant leadership may create an environment that is capable of facilitating change in suicide perceptions and improve current training.

Research Design

According to Patton (1990), there are basically two forms of research inquiry in social sciences; logical positivism and phenomenological inquiry. Patton explains logical positivism as quantitative research and phenomenological inquiry as qualitative research. These two methods have also been defined as fixed and flexible research designs (Xuehong, 2002).

These two basic designs will be evaluated for their advantages and disadvantages in the areas of basic research design, data collection methods, measurement of data and analysis of data. The combination of these methods is considered a mixed methodology approach and has recently become a more accepted form of research (Creswell, 2001). The most effective research method will be suggested in studying a police suicide awareness program.

A quantitative research design tests theories, establishes relationships, uses instruments and structured data. The researcher is viewed as an independent entity (Cooper & Schindler, 2006). A qualitative research design develops theories, describes meaning, uses observations or communication, and uses unstructured data. The researcher in this method is an integral part of the data collection process (Robson, 2002).

The advantages to a quantitative research design are the ability to explain relationships by quantifying them. Robson (2002) notes the advantage of a fixed method lies in the ability to identify patterns and relationships by interpreting statistical data collected. Fixed methods can be experimental, quasi-experimental, and non-experimental (Cooper & Schindler, 2006). The advantage of a qualitative research design approach is the flexibility and creativity permitted to the researcher (Cooper & Schindler). This flexible approach does not just show a relationship exists, but it describes it through assumptions made in grounded theory (Robson). Flexible designs include grounded theory, ethnography, and case studies (Mertens, 1998).

Some disadvantages of a fixed design are human error in data collection and analysis, cannot establish cause and effect, no control over independent variables, and the researcher cannot explain human behavior (Cooper & Schindler, 2006). Although flexible designs delve deeper into understanding relationships and human behavior, it cannot be applied to greater populations like a fixed design (Robson, 2002). A major criticism of a qualitative research design is the level of trustworthiness with respect to reliability and validity of data (Maxwell, 1992).

Data Collection Methods

Qualitative data collection methods differ from quantitative data collection in that the data is gathered using interviews instead of instruments (Rubin, 1995). Qualitative questions tend to be open ended to gain a more in-depth response from participants (Cooper & Schindler, 2006). The results from a qualitative approach are rich in detail and explain behavior, attitudes, and motivation. Qualitative research is more intensive and flexible than a quantitative approach (Robson, 2002).

Quantitative data collection utilizes survey instruments to capture empirical data. This design collects information that can be coded, validated and analyzed. An advantage to this data collection method is the ability to collect a broad range of data in a single setting; via self-administered, telephonic, internet, and in-person (Cooper & Schindler). A benefit to this collection method is the results can be generalized to represent a larger population (Berkowitz, 1996). Robson (2002) lists anonymity as an advantage to a quantitative approach which encourages honest responses to sensitive questions. However, the respondents can be affected by their memory, knowledge, personal life experience, motivation, and personality.

Berkowitz (1996) indicated qualitative data collection takes more time, thought, and effort than the collection of quantitative data. Qualitative data collection takes place in a face to face interview. The interviewer attempts to develop a rapport with the participant and verbal as well as non-verbal language is observed, recorded, and analyzed (Fontana & Frey, 1994). The interview styles include structured, semi-structured, unstructured, focused, and guided (Flick, 1998). A disadvantage to a qualitative data collection method are the results cannot be applied to general populations, data may be collected that is not relevant to the research question, very time consuming, and requires post collection categorization (Cooper & Schindler).

Analyzing Data

Once data is collected, a researcher then conducts a preliminary analysis. This initial process permits the researcher an opportunity to view relevant patterns in data (Cooper & Schindler, 2006). Quantitative data can be displayed using frequency tables, bar charts, pie charts, histograms, stem-and-leaf displays, and box plots. Qualitative data displays include flow charts, models, and graphs (Robson, 2002). Displaying data in a viewable format creates a picture for the researcher to see correlations in data, trends, and identify outliners (Luna-Reyes & Anderson, 2003).

Deciding what data analysis techniques to utilize is just as important as the development of the research question and selection of a research design. Quantitative data analysis uses descriptive statistics to describe raw data. Descriptive statistics include frequencies, percentages, measures of central tendency, and measures of variability (Cooper & Schindler, 2006). An advantage of quantitative data analysis rests on the ability to view large sets of data at one time. A strength in quantitative data analysis is the significance testing. Significance testing can be accomplished by testing differences in independent samples, dependent samples, and relationships between variables (Robson, 2002).

Disadvantages to quantitative data analysis include the inability to account for participant's motivation, lack of response to a question, and misunderstanding of the question. There is software such as SPSS available to compute statistics.
A researcher must still be able to understand the data collected, evaluate it, and interpret the data (Cooper & Schindler, 2006).

Grounded theory and ethnography are two major techniques used to analyze qualitative data (Luna-Reyes & Anderson, 2003). Grounded theory consists of identifying themes and concepts about a phenomenon. This process connects concepts to create new theories (Cooper & Schindler, 2006). Ethnography is commonly used to explain social order and add meaning to settings and situations. This technique is conducted through participant observations, interviews, diaries, and document analysis (Robson, 2002).

Advantages of qualitative analysis included in depth description of phenomena, the ability to provide individual case information, and responsive to specific needs (Cooper & Schindler, 2006). Disadvantages to qualitative data analysis are lack of generalization to a broad population, difficult to make projections or predictions, results are more easily influenced by researcher bias, and the data has lower creditability than quantitative data (Robson, 2002). A common mistake in qualitative analysis is narrowing qualitative data to the point it represents quantitative data (Luna-Reyes & Anderson, 2003).

Mixed Methods

Thomas Kuhn (1962) introduced the idea and definition of a paradigm. A paradigm essentially is a common set of standards, beliefs, values and assumptions that are accepted and acknowledged. In research there have been two dominant research paradigms; quantitative and qualitative. There have been arguments for both styles of research.

Howe (1988) supported the incompatibility thesis. This theory takes the position that quantitative and qualitative methods should not be mixed. Guba (1990) defended qualitative research method and contends that it would be impossible to blend the two research paradigms.

Quantitative and Qualitative approaches are recognized as reputable research methods, each equally as important. Mixed methods research does not replace the previously established methods. Rather, a mixed method combines the strengths in both approaches and minimizes the limitations of a singular method (Johnson & Onwuegbuzie, 2004). Both qualitative and quantitative methods have goals. Each method uses empirical observations, describe their data, and come to conclusions based on findings of their research (Sechrest & Sidana, 1995). Regardless of a research paradigm preference, each method is used to draw conclusions about participant behavior, systems, and environments. The researcher should not just ask which method to use, but how to blend the two methods to best approach the research problem, (Johnson & Onwuegbuzie, 2004).

Johnson and Onwuegbuzie (2004) classified mixed methods research as the third research paradigm. Researchers should have an understanding of various research methods. This understanding allows researchers to explore the possibility of blending attributes of different methods to conduct quality research. Hoshmand (2003) explained the benefit of mixing research methods provides the best opportunity to answering important research questions.

Mixed methods research can be developed from two major designs, mixed model, and mixed methods. Mixed model research consists of mixing qualitative and quantitative approaches across all stages of the research process. A mixed method includes blending phases of quantitative and qualitative designs. The goal of these two designs is to allow the researcher the ability to be creative and less limited by a singular design (Johnson & Onwuegbuzie, 2004). Ultimately, mixed methods create unlimited potential for future research which provides the best of both qualitative and quantitative methods (Hoshmand, 2003).

Triangulation

Triangulation builds theory from the use of multiple paradigms. Triangulation draws insights from existing data obtained from separate sources. This method combines theory, data sources and methods to study a single phenomenon (Lewis & Grimes, 1990). Denzin (1988) identified four types of triangulation; data triangulation, observer triangulation, methodological triangulation, and theory triangulation. Robson (2002) suggested triangulation can improve threats to validity. Cooper and Schindler (2006) suggested four strategies in implementing triangulation: (a) conduct qualitative and qualitative studies simultaneously; (b) while qualitative measures are ongoing quantitative data is then collected; (c) qualitative study may be followed by a quantitative study then a second qualitative study to seek greater clarification; and (d) quantitative study can follow a qualitative study.

The theory of triangulation seems to be well received among the community of scholars. However, Massey and Walford (1999) had a dissenting view on the triangulation theory. They feel the theory of triangulation is applicable solely to the physical sciences, not social sciences and applying this logic to social sciences only discredits mixed and multiple methods research. Some false assumptions of triangulation theory they identified are using a second method to prove the truth of the first method, misuse of the principle of mutual confirmation, and combining results from two different populations without statistical significance. The overall theme of this argument was to reserve the application of triangulation for land surveying and physical sciences, and not social science research (Massey & Walford). Although they present a credible argument, there seems to be more literature supporting the theory of triangulation than dispelling it.

Summary

This chapter covers the seminal research conducted on the sensitive topic of police suicide. A background of the problem as well as current issues is discussed. The officers' role and pressure to conform to the profession of law enforcement is identified. Issues related to training and current training offered by other agencies is identified. Leadership styles were compared and as well as the strengths and weaknesses of each. Finally, a critical examination of research methodologies is conducted and the strengths and weaknesses of each identified. The next chapter outlines the research methodology selected for this study.

CHAPTER 3. METHODOLOGY

The alarming high rate of police officer suicides in America, coupled with the lack of formal training on the problem, warrants further investigation, and formal research.

This study aims to provide law enforcement leaders insight into this complicated and often ignored problem. The sensitivity of the subject matter presents a difficult challenge in researching this problem. A strong and structured organizational culture also present challenges in gathering information from members of the law enforcement community. The lack of formal documentation on a national level makes it difficult to determine how serious this problem may be.

Previous studies have focused on the number of completed suicides and have compared them to different professions, the general public, and various demographic categories. This study is unique because it measures the officer's perception on suicide, identifies circumstances which may cause an officer to consider suicide as a possible option, and identifies if additional training in the academy and annual in-service on suicide awareness is warranted.

The intent of this study was to investigate the relationship between the perceptions of suicide by police officers, identify what factors may lead them to consider suicide, and uncover additional risk factors or warnings signs related to suicidal ideation. This information is relevant for supervisors to implement suicide awareness training and to potentially identify officers in need of assistance.

The purpose of research is to increase the depth of a specific topic, exploration, and the development of knowledge creation (Robson, 2002). Good research should be conducted with sound reasoning (Cooper & Schindler, 2006). Robson explains that research should be conducted with a scientific attitude and carried out systematically, skeptically, and ethically. Even in well designed projects, researchers must be cautious of their own bias based on their own prejudices of which they may not be cognizant of (Hoadley, 2004).

Trochin (2006) defined a good research design as the glue that holds all other elements together. The selection of a specific research method will have a critical role in the type of information gathered, method of collection, measurement of data, and analysis of data.

This study is designed to measure the perceptions of sworn law enforcement officers, positive or negative related to attitudes toward suicide. The importance of this subject is to address the problem of police suicide from a human resources perspective. Understanding the attitudes toward suicide will enable leaders to better understand the police suicide problem, develop future suicide awareness, and suicide prevention training for police officers.

The research questions for this study are as follows:

1. Is there a difference in suicide perceptions based on geographical locations, specifically west coast compared to east coast?

2. Is there a difference in suicide perceptions among demographic categories such as gender, time of service, rank, and job description?

3. What circumstances are more likely to make an officer consider suicide or not consider suicide as an option?

4. Is there a difference in suicide prevention training based on geographical locations?

5. Is there a need to improve upon suicide prevention training?

Research Design

The National Police Suicide Foundation recently administered the Suicide Attitude Questionnaire, (SUIATT) to various police departments across the country. This research intends to utilize the raw data collected from the foundation to compare and contrast two groups. The two groups consist of an agency from the west coast and an agency from the east coast.

The benefit of using this previously collected data is the data comes from a reputable source, it is cost effective, time efficient, and manageable. It would not be feasible for the researcher to travel across the country and collect data on this large of a scale.

The sample was obtained from officers who attended training given by the National Police Suicide Foundation. The officers voluntarily participated in the anonymous survey and vary in rank, experience, and demographics. An equal number of surveys will be used to compare the two groups.

Instrumentation

The Suicide Attitude Questionnaire was developed by Diekstra and Kerkhof in 1989. This instrument is intended to measure attitudes of professionals toward suicide among strangers, loved ones, and social groups under certain circumstances. The instrument is a 93 item questionnaire which utilizes a 5 point Likert scale from A to E. The instrument takes approximately 15-20 minutes to administer (Diekstra & Kerkhof 1988).

The instrument originally was tested using the general population which netted 712 respondents. The instrument test-re-test reliability was reported very high (r=.82). The instrument has been used by other professions to measure perceptions of suicide. Other instruments have been developed to measure attitudes towards suicide, but do not have as high reliability, and are not as in-depth as the SUIATT.

A demographic data sheet was attached to the SUIATT in order to collect pertinent data about the participants. The demographic data is formatted in a multiple choice fashion. This information includes age, gender, educational level, ethnicity, religion, experience, and asks to give a percentage value of responsibility for officer suicide. These questions are necessary to answer the research questions in this study.

Data Collection

Permission was requested and granted from Dr. Kerkhof, one of the creators of the SUIATT. He is currently a Psychology Professor in the Netherlands.

The instrument was administered by the Executive Director of the National Police Suicide Foundation, Robert Douglas Jr. Permission was requested and granted to utilize the data he collected from participants attending training. The participants consist of sworn law enforcement professionals that vary in experience, job description, demographic background, and geographic locations.

Data Analysis

Measurement is the process of observing and capturing data that are collected as part of a research design (Robson, 2002). The process can be divided into a three part process by assigning numbers to empirical events, objects, properties, and activities in a structured manner. The three part process includes: (a) selecting observable events; (b) developing a set of mapping rules; and (c) applying the mapping rules to each observable category (Cooper & Schindler, 2006).

Quantitative measurement comes from a statistically significant sample of a population, called a sample size (Chan, 2003). The data collected can be used to measure consumer behavior, knowledge, opinion and attitudes. These questions answer how much, how often, how many, when, and who (Cooper & Schindler, 2006). The data collected in a fixed method can be categorized into nominal, ordinal, interval and ratio data. The data is coded numerically and a researcher can easily see relationships and differences which can be reproduced (Robson, 2002).

Scoring of the instrument includes taking a sum total of each scale response. The A to E is converted into 1 to 5 to accommodate statistical analysis. Sixty-four items, a higher score indicates a negative response. Twenty-five items have a reverse scoring, in that a higher response yields a more positive attitude towards suicide. The remaining four items require a written response. This research will focus on specific items on the instrument to measures perceptions relevant to the profession of law enforcement. Not all items on the instrument will be scored.

The data will be coded and entered into SPSS software for statistical analysis. Frequency distributions and descriptive data will be viewed to gain an overall understanding of the data and identify any outliners or errors in data entry.

The data will be statistically analyzed using nonparametric tests and bivariate correlation procedure. These statistical tests will examine relationships between attitudes towards suicide as collected by the SUAITT instrument, and various demographic data provided by the participant.

The independent variable is attitude, which can be measured as positive or negative. The dependent variable is the personal and professional perception towards suicide as indicated on the SUIATT instrument. A sample correlation may be a participant who has a family history of suicide, or a participant whose partner committed suicide may show negative perceptions towards suicide. A positive perception may be recorded by a participant who had previous suicidal ideation, sought help and is no longer contemplating suicide. The variables can be identified by the responses provided through the SUIATT instrument.

The final analysis conducted is the Spearman Correlation Coefficient Test. This analysis focuses on demographic variables to determine if these variables have a relationship with an officer's attitude towards suicide as measured by the SUIATT instrument. This analysis will also examine if there is a difference between perceptions, positive or negative, among officers in different geographic locations, east coast versus west coast. If a measurable difference is detected, then factors leading to these differences will be closely examined.

Sample

The sample consists of sworn law enforcement officers who attended suicide prevention training. This is considered a convenient sample. This research includes using anonymous secondary data.

The participants attended formal training given by the National Police Suicide Foundation. While at this training, they voluntarily participated in an anonymous survey on suicide perceptions.

This research is designed to utilize existing data with no personal identifiable information available. The need for a consent/assent is not necessary for this study.

Limitations

Limitations to this study include the methodology. Although quantitative methods can be more statistically significant and have greater reliability than qualitative methods, the information can be restrictive. Qualitative research delves deeper into understanding relationships and correlations between variables. Qualitative results may show that a relationship exists but does not qualify why it exists. The subject matter is very sensitive in nature. Officers may be reluctant and suspicious to answer honestly in fear of negative repercussions from their respective organizations.

Existing data on officer suicides is another limitation to this study. Currently there are no local, state or federal requirements that accurately memorialize officer suicides or demand agencies to report them. This discrepancy is noted in the difference in documented suicides by the Federal Uniform Crime Reports as compared to validated officer suicides recorded by the National Police Suicide Foundation.

The population is limited as well. Until the data is received, it is difficult to determine if it is equally distributed and an accurate representation of a specific population. This study may be able to identify general assumptions but it may not be a valid source to identify future predictors of behavior for larger populations.

This study measures the officers' perception on the date the instrument was taken. It is limited to how the officer feels that day, unknown factors such as personal or professional problems cannot be identified. Family history in coping with stress, previous family member suicides or personal suicide attempts is unknown, unless disclosed through the SUIATT instrument.

Expected Findings

The researcher's hypotheses for this study are as follows:

1. There will be a difference in suicide perceptions based on geographical locations, specifically west coast compared to east coast. This may be based on training, education, and religious influences.

2. A measurable difference will be detected in suicide perceptions among demographic categories such as gender, time of service, and job description.

3. Specific circumstances will be identified when officers are more likely to consider suicide or not consider suicide as an option.

4. There will be a significant deficit identified in police suicide awareness training in both groups examined.

5. A need to implement and possibly require suicide training to all levels of the organization may be identified.

Ethical Considerations

The participants individually will not benefit from this study. However, this study hopes to contribute to the academic body of knowledge, resulting in a benefit to the law enforcement community and may potentially prevent additional suicides.

No risks or harm to participants are identified in this study. Participants voluntarily completed a survey during voluntary training. No personal identifiable data, agency affiliation or training sign in roosters were viewed by the researcher. The participants are completely anonymous to the researcher.

Proper security measures are being utilized to securely preserve the original data for a period of seven years from date of publication.

CHAPTER 4. RESULTS

Data

Once the data was received, the instruments were assigned an identification number because no demographic information on participants was obtained. This was done to preserve anonymity. The data was coded numerically and entered into an Excel spreadsheet. This coded data was then imported into SPSS statistical software for data analysis.

Initially, complete descriptive statistics with frequencies were run for all the variables. This function was conducted to view the distribution of variables, identify any errors in data entry, determine if there was any missing data, and finally observe if the data was equally distributed.

The variables investigated are based on age, gender, religion, time of service, and previous training on the subject of suicide prevention. These variables are then compared to responses to the SUIATT instrument to determine perceptions on suicide, circumstances leading to suicidal ideation, and perceptions on suicide prevention efforts in the United States.

Demographics

The participants for this study voluntarily completed the SUIATT instrument administered by the National Police Suicide Foundation, during the winter of 2006. The average time to complete the instrument was 20 minutes. The sample consists of a convenient sample of 75 participants from two groups, police officers from the west coast, and police officers from the east coast. The two regions were selected to determine if there where any differences based on geographical locations. The names of the agencies will remain anonymous to further protect the anonymity of participants.

Table 1 displays the distribution of demographic data for both groups. These variables include gender, age, race/ethnicity, and education. The data revealed the groups were equally represented. The participants include 20 females and 55 males in each group. The east coast participants consisted of thirteen African Americans, one American Indian, one Asian, 59 Caucasians, and zero Latino officers. The west coast participants were made up of four African Americans, three American Indians, Zero Asian, 55 Caucasians, and thirteen Latino officers.

Age of the participants varied among the groups. The largest representation for the east coast participants was the 40-44 age range with 18 participants. The west coast had the most representation in the 50-54 age range with 22 participants. The east coast group had greater distribution in the age range with seven officers represented in the 25-29 categories. All of the west coast officers were 30 years old and above.

The east coast participants had more formal education representation than the west coast officers. The west coast officers consisted of 37.3% high school graduates, where the east coast officers had over 79% graduate from college and one PhD graduate. This may be a result in a difference of entrance requirements for police officers. These requirements often vary among agencies. Advanced degrees were represented greater within the east coast participants. There were fourteen advanced degrees recorded compared to four in the west coast group.

Table 1. Participants Demographic Data for East Coast and west coast officers (N=150).

Variable	Frequency		Percentage	
	East	West	East	West

Variable	East	West	East	West
Gender				
Male	55	55	73.3	73.3
Female	20	20	26.7	26.7
Age				
20-24	0	0	0.0	0.0
25-29	7	0	9.3	0.0
30-34	11	12	14.7	16.0
35-39	15	20	20.0	26.7
40-44	18	14	24.0	18.7
50-54	14	22	18.7	29.3
>55	10	7	13.3	9.3
Race/Ethnicity				
African American	13	4	17.3	5.3
American Indian	1	3	1.3	4.0
Asian	1	0	1.3	0.0
Caucasian	59	55	78.7	73.3
Latino	0	13	0.0	17.3
Education				
High School	16	28	21.3	37.3
AA/AS	12	23	16.0	30.7
BA/BS	33	20	44.0	26.7
MA/MS	13	4	17.3	5.3
JD/PhD	1	0	1.3	0.0

Findings

Hypotheses 1.

There will be a difference in suicide perceptions based on geographical locations, specifically west coast compared to east coast. This may be based on training, education, and religious influences.

In order to determine perceptions on suicide, three specific factors from the SUIATT were analyzed using questions one, twenty-six, and ninety-four; (a) how likely is the officer to end their life by suicide, (b) how does the officer feel about suicide, and (c) does the officer feel they have a right to commit suicide? Each of these factors was analyzed against a demographic variable which includes training, education, and religious influences.

Factor 1: How likely is the officer to end their life by suicide? The participants had five options for this question, on a five point Likert scale; (a) very likely, (b) fairly likely, (c) don't know, (d) fairly unlikely, and (e) unlikely. In both groups, one officer indicated it was very likely they would end their life by suicide. Neither officer had previous suicide prevention training in the academy. Education was not a factor in this decision either; the west coast officer had a high school diploma while the east coast officer indicated they completed a bachelor's degree. Both officers declared their faith as Catholics.

The west coast group indicated 90.7% were very unlikely to end their life by suicide and the east coast group recorded 85.3%. The east coast officers indicated that 24% of them were trained in the academy on officer suicide awareness, compared to 96% of the west coast officers not being trained.

Factor 2: How does the officer feel about suicide? The participants had five options for this question, on a five point Likert scale; (a) I don't know, (b) It is a fairly bad thing, (c) It is a bad thing, (d) It is one of the worst things that can happen, and (e) It is the worst thing that can happen. The west coast showed a less negative perception towards suicide for this factor. A total of 68% of the west coast respondents had a positive score for this factor compared to 8% of the east coast officers.

Forty-seven percent of the east coast officers selected a neutral response to this factor and 29% indicated a negative response. This factor indicated a high correlation between education and perceptions for the east coast group, the significance level, (2-sided) for the east coast group was .744, which indicates the relationship was not statistically significant.

Factor 3: Does the officer feel they have a right to commit suicide? The respondents again had five selections to chose from; (a) always, (b) most of the time, (c) Don't know/no opinion, (d) sometimes, and (e) never. Both groups were very similar in the negative response to suicide for this question. Always was selected by thirteen west coast officers and twelve east coast officers. The east coast had a 48% response rate with suicide never being a viable option, compared to 40% by the west coast group. There was a significant relationship with respect to education measured at .222 with a positive correlation of .143. In both groups, the results indicate religious preferences did not have a positive correlation on considering suicide as an option. Twice as many officers without suicide awareness training indicated they always have a right to commit suicide.

Hypotheses 2.

A measurable difference will be detected in suicide perceptions among demographic categories such as gender, time of service, and job description. The factors in this hypotheses are identical to those in hypotheses one. The significant difference is three different demographic variables are analyzed.

In order to determine perceptions on suicide three factors were analyzed; (a) how likely is the officer to end their life by suicide, (b) how does the officer feel about suicide, and (c) does the officer feel they have a right to commit suicide? Each of these factors was analyzed against a demographic variable which includes gender, time of service, and job description.

Factor 1: How likely is the officer to end their life by suicide? The participants had five options for this question, on a five point Likert scale; (a) very likely, (b) fairly likely, (c) don't know, (d) fairly unlikely, and (e) unlikely. In both groups, one officer indicated it was very likely they would end their life by suicide. There was not a significant correlation between age and factor 1. The significance level was lower than .05 and therefore rejects any correlation between these two variables. The west coast officer who identified he was very likely to consider suicide as an option was in the 40-44 age range, with 20-25 years of experience, and is working in patrol. The east coast officer with the same response reported his age as 55 and over, over 25 years of experience, and is working in an administrative position.

Factor 2: How does the officer feel about suicide? The participants had five options for this question, on a five point Likert scale; (a) I don't know, (b) It is a fairly bad thing, (c) It is a bad thing, (d) It is one of the worst things that can happen, and (e) It is the worst thing that can happen. The east coast group had the largest representation of participants working patrol, n=24. Fourteen officers had a positive perception for this factor, eight were neutral and two were negative. The years of experience groups with the most positive perception for this factor were the 11-15 and 16-20 years of experience groups. The variable age showed a positive trend between ages 25-34, neutral for ages 35-39, followed by a negative trend for the older ages groups age 40 and above.

The west coast group had the largest representation of participants working patrol, n=50. Thirty officers had a positive perception for this factor, eighteen were neutral and two were negative. The years of experience groups with the most positive perception for this factor were the 6-10 and 11-15 years of experience groups. The variable age showed a positive trend between ages 25-34, neutral for ages 35-39, followed by a negative trend for the older age groups age 40 and above, this trend was similar to the east coast group.

Factor 3: Does the officer feel they have a right to commit suicide? The respondents again had five selections to chose from; (a) always, (b) most of the time, (c) Don't know/no opinion, (d) sometimes, and (e) never. Age was not a factor in deciding the right to commit suicide. However in both groups there was an observable difference in the years of experience categories. The west coast group showed a trend with the greater the officer's experience; the less right a person had to commit suicide. The significance level between these two variables was .180. The east coast group varied in responses based on years of experience. The variable current assignment varied between the two groups. The east coast group patrol officer noted less freedom in having a right to commit suicide than the administrators in the group. The west coast officers were opposite the east coast officers in this factor. Their patrol officers responded with greater frequency when it comes to the right to commit suicide as compared to the administration. The west coast group showed a greater correlation between current assignment and the right to choose suicide as an option, p value = .816 compared to .318 for the east coast group.

Hypotheses 3.

Specific circumstances will be identified when officers are more likely to consider suicide or not consider suicide as an option.

The participants were asked; under what circumstances might you commit suicide? A series of circumstances followed, see table 2. The participants had five options for this question, on a five point Likert scale; (a) Definitely yes, (b) Probably yes, (c) Maybe/Maybe not, (d) Probably no, and (e) definitely no. To compute the percentages, the frequencies of positive responses were combined to provide a final outcome. Table 2, outlines the percentages for both groups. The variables are listed side by side to make comparing the two groups more convenient.

Table 2. Participant's responses to suicide as an option.

Variable	East	West
If you were old and crippled?	13.3%	10.7%
If you suffered from chronic pain?	20.0%	8.0%
If you had AIDS?	28.0%	10.7%
If you became severely disabled?	30.7%	14.7%
If you became unemployed?	26.7%	18.7%
If you had a handicapped child?	29.3%	0.0%
If admitted to a mental hospital?	18.7%	16.0%
If impossible to have children?	24.0%	10.7%
If you suffered an incurable disease?	24.0%	12.0%
Person most dear to you dies?	25.3%	8.0%
If you don't find a life partner?	29.3%	0.0%
If you had killed someone else?	29.3%	20.0%
If you had Alzheimer's disease?	24.0%	13.3%

Hypotheses 4.

There will be a significant deficit identified in police suicide awareness training in both groups examined. A frequency description was conducted to determine if the participants were previously trained in the academy and during in-service. The information was documented on the demographic sheet attached to the SUIATT instrument.

The east coast officers had more diversity in jurisdiction. The sample consisted of federal, state, county, and municipal officers. Seventy-four percent of the participants indicated they did not have previous training in the academy or during annual in-service training. Of the officers who did have formal training, three were federal, three state, three county and nine municipal officers. The west coast group responded that 96% of the participants had no academy training, and 90.7% received no formal training on police suicide during annual in-service updates. This sample consisted solely of state officers.

Hypotheses 5.

A need to implement and possibly require suicide training to all levels of the organization may be identified. A frequency distribution was conducted to determine if the participants perceived suicide prevention efforts in the United States in a positive or negative light. This information was obtained from responses in the SUIATT instrument.

The participants had five options for this question, on a five point Likert scale; (a) very negative, (b) fairly negative, (c) don't know/no opinion, (d) fairly positive, and (e) very positive. The negative and positive responses were combined to measure perceptions. The do not know/no opinion was classified as a neutral position for suicide prevention efforts in the United States. The results for the east coast showed a 41.3% negative perception, 40.0% neutral, and 18.7% positive. The west coast participants showed 48% negative perceptions, 28% neutral, and 24% positive. Figures 1 and 2 show this data in a bar graph.

Summary

This chapter defined the research questions, and provided the expected findings for each. The results of the data collected were described and tables and figures were generated to accompany the data. The final chapter includes discussion of results, implications, and recommendations for future research.

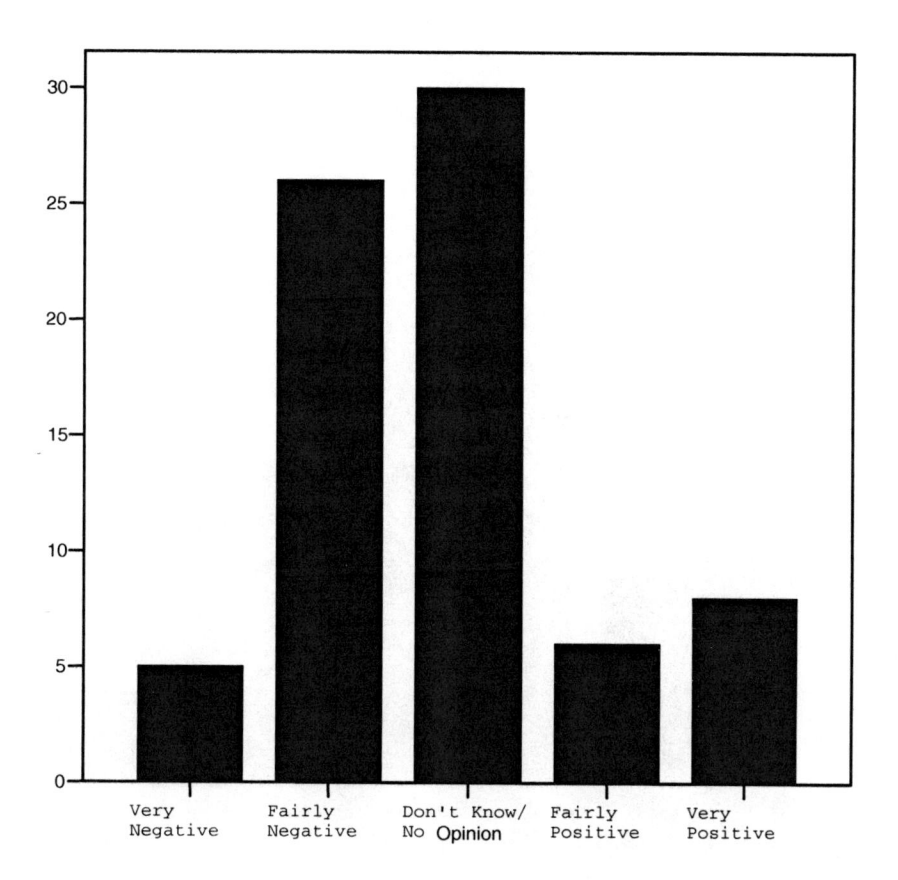

Figure 1.

Opinion on suicide prevention efforts
in U.S.
East Coast Officers
(N=75)

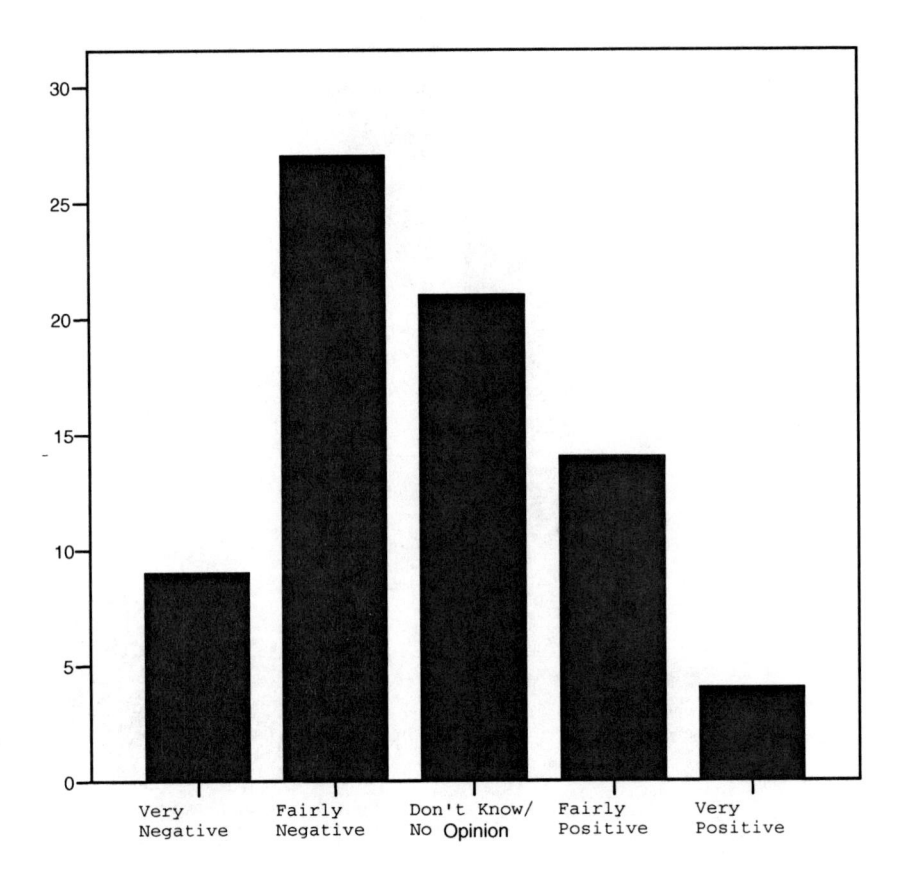

Figure 2.

Opinion on suicide prevention efforts in U.S
West Coast officers.
(N=75)

CHAPTER 5. DISCUSSION, IMPLICATIONS, AND RECOMMENDATIONS

Discussion

Participants for this study included 40 females and 110 males representing two groups, west coast and east coast sworn police officers. The participants while attending training on police suicide voluntarily completed the Suicide Attitude Questionnaire administered by Robert Douglas Jr., Executive Director of the National Police Suicide Foundation.

This research was exploratory in nature and sought to examine a relationship between attitudes toward suicide and demographic variables between the two groups. In addition, participant's responses were closely examined to identify risk factors and warnings signs of potential suicidal ideation. Finally, results were examined to determine if training was recommended for officers in one or both groups for subordinates and supervisors.

In addition to the results portion of the study other noteworthy information was observed. Specially, the difference in number of suicides reported in each group, previous suicide attempts documented, preferred method of death if you were to commit suicide, and who was identified as most responsible for the act of suicide.

The east coast group was more diverse in terms of jurisdiction. This group consisted of a medley of officers from federal through municipal agencies. The participants were asked to write how many suicides their agency had experienced in the past 5 years. The east coast group ranged from zero to six officers killed in the past five years. Fifty-three officers in the east coast group reported no suicides in the past five years. Fifteen officers reported one, four officers documented three, and one officer indicated six suicides in the past five years for their agency.

The west coast group consisted of officers from the same agency, a state law enforcement entity. Two factors were very noticeable from this statistical analysis. The first factor was how many deaths this agency suffered. The second factor was how varied the responses were from members of the same agency.

The west coast group reports ranged from seven to as high as thirty officers deceased as a result of suicide in the past five years. Most of the participants wrote the number of deaths reported in the past seventeen months. This would be a time frame between 2004 and 2006. Twenty three officers reported 14 suicide deaths, 26 officers indicated 15 deaths in 17 months, seven officers listed seventeen deaths, three officers reported 18 suicides, and four officers documented over 20 deaths in a 17 month period.

Comparing the two groups and their loss to suicide it was surprising that the west coast group was more satisfied with suicide prevention efforts in the United States than the east coast group. Both agencies reported very low when it came to previous training on suicide prevention in the academy and annual pre-service training. Neither group reported having a funeral policy in place for officers who commit suicide.

The next factor viewed was the number of suicide attempts between the two groups. The east coast group reported two officers who attempted suicide more than once. This group also had four officers who attempted suicide once. The west coast group had two participants report attempting suicide once and 73 participants never attempt suicide.

The groups varied in which methods they would prefer if they committed suicide. The figures below provide a visual display of the results. In both group women preferred the less violent means of death, pills or poison when compared to their male counter parts that chose guns. One officer wrote, suicide by cop was his preferred method.

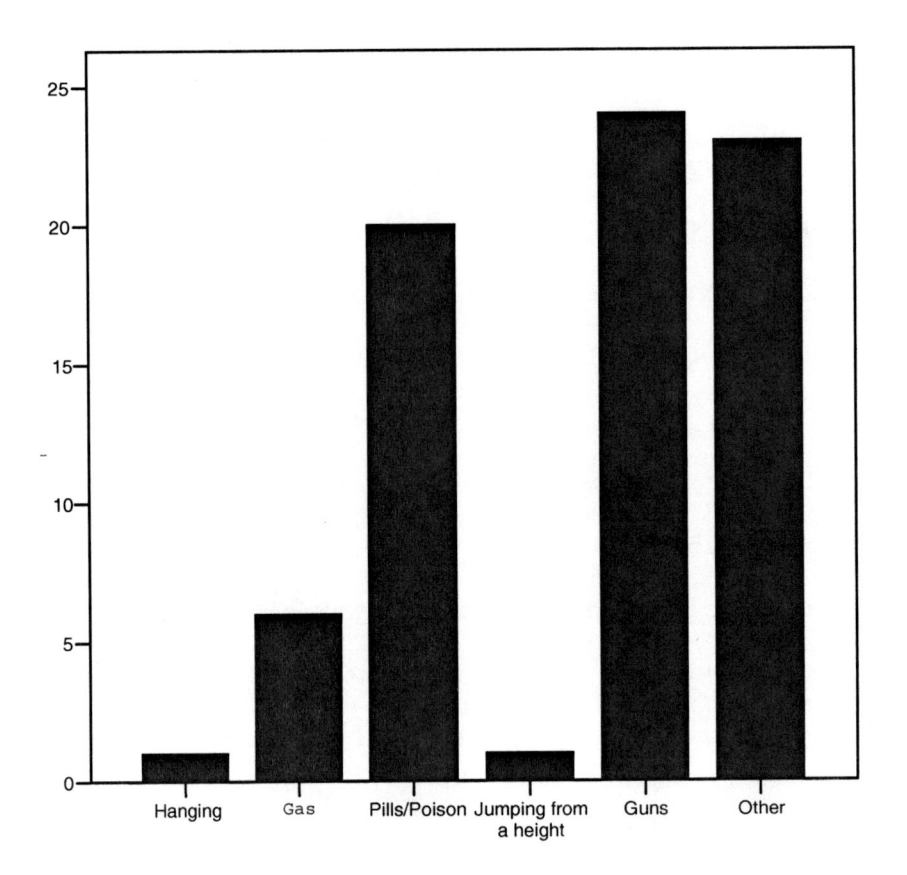

Figure 3.

Your method of choice for committing suicide?
East Coast Officers
N=75

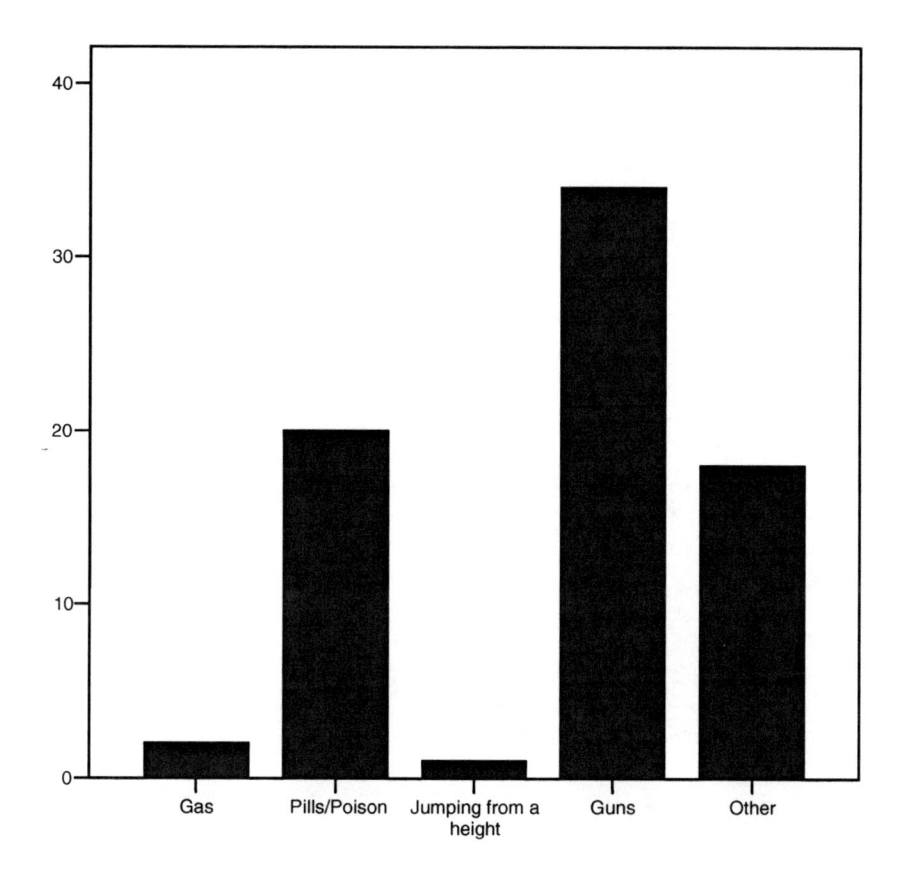

Figure 4.

Your method of choice for committing suicide?
West Coast Officers
N=75

The final question on the demographic data sheet asked officers to provide a percentage value for the amount of responsibility when an officer commits suicide. The options available were; (a) officer, (b) job, (c) relationship, (d) administration, (e) training, and (f) agency. Sixteen participants from the east coast group list the officer as being solely responsible for suicide and 56 reported a combination of factors. Ninety percent of the west coast group listed the officer as solely responsible, and three participants indicted a combination of factors.

Implications

Based on the results of the study, it appears that leaders have much room for improvement with respect to implementing training, and effective policy for suicide prevention. It was alarming that the west coast group documented an average of 19 suicides in an 18 month period; yet still do not have a formal police suicide awareness model. Ninety six percent of their officers documented never being trained in police suicide.

Leaders must be critically reflective in their leadership style, and be willing to serve the members beneath them. Being a critically reflective leader demonstrates characteristics of a leader who is willing to change for the good of the organization and the members following them. Strong leadership and mandatory suicide prevention training are the keys to a successful suicide prevention model, which may reduce officer suicide rates in America. This was evident in the implementation of the suicide prevention efforts by the United State Air Force. The Air Force implemented a holistic suicide awareness program which trained command staff through family members and documented a significant reduction in suicides.

Brookfield (1998) identified four lenses of critical reflection, lens of our own autobiographical experiences, lens of the learner's eye, lens of a colleague's perception, and the lens of theoretical literature. Brookfield's theory of critical reflection was created for teachers to discover and research the assumptions they make about teaching and learning. Utilizing the practice of critical reflection will help teachers make more informed decisions, understand their actions, and make personal improvements in their teaching style and learning environment.

Leadership plays a critical role in shaping the organizational culture of a police agency (Greene, Alpert, & Styles, 1992). The same principles of a critically reflective teacher will be applied to becoming a critically reflective leader as a law enforcement executive. The four lenses of critical reflection are analyzed and evaluated on how a leader can use critical reflection to influence the organizational culture of a law enforcement agency.

Background

Elias and Merriam (1995) traced critical reflection back twenty-five centuries to Confucius in China. Its original form was called humanism and was a process of self criticism characterized by the metaphor of "inner digging and drilling." They believed learning could not take place without silent reflection. Other theorists use reflection as a means of expanding self understanding, some are Festinger's (1957) cognitive dissonance theory, Kuhn's (1962) paradigm shifts, Mesirow's (1978) theory of reflectivity, and currently Brookfield's (1998) theory of critical reflection.

The theory of critical reflection has been applied mainly to adult education. King (2004) stated that the theory of critical reflection is too narrowly focused. There is a need to broaden the theory into different academic disciplines to foster greater reflection and personal development. The process of critical reflection leads to the creation of new knowledge.

Critical Reflection

Mezirow (1990) suggested using critical reflection to establish if prior education and experience is acceptable under present circumstances. A non-reflective person engages in habitual actions without an understanding why decisions are made. Mezirow noted critical reflection leads to transformative learning. Transformative learning reflectively shapes attitudes, beliefs, and opinions. Being critically reflective describes how we perceive, understand and feel about events. This practice provides a new understanding why decisions are made and the ability to observe and critically analyze their effectiveness.

Critical reflection is a systematic and deliberate attempt to understand personal assumptions. Brookfield (1998) identified three reasons to explore critical reflection. First, critical reflection encourages taking informed actions and making educated decisions. Second, critical reflection stems from and facilitates critical thinking. Allowing others to understand the process of critical reflection helps them understand the thought process behind decisions and actions. Third, critical reflection creates new knowledge, practices, and a personal understanding of new assumptions.

Law enforcement executives must be aware of the significant influence their authority and leadership style has on the entire organization. Bennett and Hess (1996) indicated police managers at all levels must possess specific skills and tools to be effective. Managers must be forward thinkers, make complex decisions, and have broad perspectives. The police agency must not be viewed as a separate entity, rather as a part of society. Critical reflection provides an executive with tools to measure their personal growth as a leader as well as measuring the effectiveness of the organization from others viewpoints.

Organizational Culture

Kluckhon (1949) described culture as a set of traditional ways of thinking, feeling, and reacting in a particular society. Organizational culture expands this definition to describe the culture of a system. Organizational culture defines shared ideas, customs, traditions, values, and influences how the group interacts and behaves. Within a culture a subculture can emerge which consists of a smaller sample of a population. A subculture in a law enforcement agency can be formal. This subculture can be in the form of a task force or specialized unit which has their own set of norms, values, and customs (Harrison, 1998). An informal group can develop from the larger population creating a subculture within the organization.

Understanding the existing culture of a police agency can assist an executive leader in creating policy, developing strategic planning, and sharing vision. Drummond (1976) described how the assimilation to the police culture begins in the selection process, standardized academy training, and continues through field training. The environment is a quasi-military style with a centralized chain of command, uniforms, and clear-cut roles and responsibilities. This quasi-military environment creates isolation from others, solidarity within the agency, and an adversarial mentality towards the public and administration (Harrison, 1998).

The police culture has been criticized for deviant behavior, loss of ethics, abuse of power, and selective use of discretion. Understanding the ability to reflect upon the goals and mission of the agency a leader can be influential in using the ingrained values of the culture to stimulate organizational improvement and growth (Harrison, 1998). The first step in creating a positive shift in an organizational culture consists of conducting a critical reflection by the executive in accordance with Brookfield's four lenses of critical reflection.

Lens of Autobiographical Experiences

Brookfield (1998), explained that our personal experiences have a profound and long lasting influence. Many law enforcement executives encounter organizational resistance when implementing change in their organization's culture. They too were assimilated into the culture during their career and the same culture they are trying to change is the vehicle that placed them in a leadership position.

The law enforcement executive must reflect on what events in his or her background have influenced the leadership style they employ. This activity of reflection is also known as self-awareness. Self-awareness allows a leader to understand his or her values, identify where they fit in the organizations mission, and identify the root of their personal assumptions (Goleman, 1998).

The risk in critical reflection from autobiographical experiences and self awareness is coming to the conclusion the way things were being conducted was not always proper. The leader may experience a sense of responsibility for organizational problems (Brookfield, 1998). The benefit of critical reflection is for the leader to grow in his or her leadership style. Critical reflection creates a mechanism of checks and balances to periodically evaluate the effectiveness of a leader and leads to conformity in the agencies values and mission statements.

Lens of Learner's eye

The lens of the learner's eye according to Brookfield (1998) is the perspective from which the student is the stakeholder in an educational environment. The stakeholders for a police agency are the citizens served, civilian support staff, family members of the department, members of government, and community leaders. Reflection through lens of other members of the department is discussed through the lens of colleague's perception.

Critical reflection in this area can assist an executive to open lines of communication with the stakeholders, identify problems, and create new ideas. Brookfield (1998) noted whenever a teacher received feedback from students; this reflection caused the teacher to learn something about them. The same can be accomplished by a law enforcement executive. The executive through this form of reflection could better serve the community and properly deploy resources to solve problems.

The greatest benefit of this lens is the comparison of the organizational goals and the community's needs. Goleman (1998) indicated a leader who practices self awareness is capable of constructive criticism. Leaders possessing a strong sense of self awareness are honest with themselves and to others. Self awareness helps a leader identify their emotions, strengths, weaknesses, goals, and motives.

Lens of Colleague's Perception

Lens of a colleague's perspective will encompass not only colleagues from the same agency but from all levels of the law enforcement community. Brookfield (1998) pointed out that critical reflection often begins alone, but is most effective when completed in a collective fashion. This approach is new for law enforcement because the profession breeds isolation. The isolation not only exists between the police and the community, it exists within sections of the same agency and isolation between jurisdictional lines among other agencies (Harrison, 1998).

Internally a law enforcement executive can learn from feedback received from other members of command staff as well as line members, and civilian support staff. The use of a 360-degree feedback is one instrument that could assist in the critical reflection process. Velsor and Leslie (1991) noted annual performance reviews are subjective and insufficient. The use of a 360-degree evaluation provides a perspective from multiple views. The previous appraisal system was a form of downward communication. A 360-degree instrument collects data from a variety of sources and the target of the instrument is evaluated from different view points. Kouzes and Posner (2003) created the Leadership Practices Inventory. The inventory solicits responses from managers, co-workers, direct reports, and others to rate a leader's effectiveness. A scale is used to measure how often the leader engages in the behavior described. The Leadership Practices Inventory is a reliable instrument that is manageable to administer and provides a leader with insight on their personal strengths and weaknesses.

Externally, a leader can learn from attending conferences with other executives, specialized training, and joining professional associations. Conferences are hosted by larger agencies such as the Federal Bureau of Investigation. The FBI also hosts a specialized leadership training academy, called the National Academy. Professional associations could be fraternal such as a local union or specific to rank like the International Association for Chiefs of Police (Bennett & Hess, 1996).

Similar to reflections gained through the perception of self and stakeholders, information gained from colleagues can have a two-fold effect on a leader. In one instance a leader may gain momentum and motivation from the responses received and feels comfortable in their leadership style and direction the organization is going. On the other hand, a leader may not feel comfortable with the results received from colleagues. It is essential that a leader be open-minded to the feedback received from colleagues and not take the information personal. This new information can lead to new growth in the organization, improved employee satisfaction, and increase the quality of services provided. Velsor and Leslie (1991) characterize strong leaders as willing to seek feedback both positive and negative.

Lens of Theoretical Literature

Theoretical literature review is a process of investigation and critical thinking where social phenomenon is explored. The process consists of classifying, comparing, contrasting, and collaborating information (Miles & Huberman, 1994). Cresswell (2001) defined the purpose of a literature review as a benchmark for comparing results of previous research and provides a conceptual framework in establishing the importance of the topic studied.

The benefit of reflection through the lens of theory is benchmarking. Benchmarking in a process of evaluating what standards are acceptable, identifying best practices, and determining who the best is at what they do. Brookfield (1998) noted existing literature is helpful to teachers to analyze dilemmas and problems. Existing literature keeps teachers current in styles, practices, and application of theory.

Law enforcement executives are no different. It is the responsibility of a law enforcement executive to remain current on changing laws and practices in a professional police agency. Bennett and Hess (1996) noted change in a police agency is inevitable and no person or organization can stop it. Reflecting on the events of September 11, 2001, the profession of law enforcement has changed forever.

Brookfield (1998) explained that literature plays an important role in critical reflection by bringing understanding to our actions and provides the ability of describing and labeling them. Literature can help explain why events occur and prevent executives from feeling personally responsible for everything that occurs in their agency. A literature review can also be a source of comfort. Reading how other executives handle problems within their agency, could lead to a learning experience, without going through the event personally.

Leaders must be capable of transforming in order to reach excellence. Their subordinates must be considered as valuable as their stakeholders (Taborada, 2000). King (2005) described the theoretical process of critical reflection as an awakening that causes one to question their beliefs, values, and assumptions. The process of critical reflection creates new understanding, empowers those who reflect, and improves confidence in decision making. A leader who is truly effective has an elevated degree of self awareness and understands where they are headed and why (Goleman, 1998). Self awareness provides a leader with an understanding of their emotions, decision making process, theoretical basis, and their influence on others.

Characteristics of organizational culture in a law enforcement agency are not all bad. Officers have a tendency to isolate themselves from previous friends, loved ones, and the community. This social isolation is a defense mechanism that keeps officers safe in the line of duty from perceived dangers, societal rejection, and often causes them to become suspicious of others (Drummond, 1976).

Critical reflection from a law enforcement executive can assist them in learning about their personal leadership style, understanding theory behind their actions, and continuously strive to improve the organization. Harrison (1998) suggested that leaders would be foolish to ignore cultural implications when creating policy. Critical reflection creates ownership in an organization and encourages participative decision making. Including the community and other stakeholders in critical reflection stimulates collaboration with citizens and reduces isolation. Ultimately, critical reflection sets the stage for open communication, teamwork, and personal as well as professional growth (Brookfield, 1998).

Recommendations

The recommendations based on this study include improvement to current training, and implementing training if it does not exist. Leaders at all levels need the skills to identify officers at risk and understand the resources available to them. Over one-half of the east coast group identified a combination of factors that lead an officer to make suicide the final answer. Supervisors need to possess the ability to effectively identify warning signs and risk factors in their member. If a supervisor determines and officer may be at risk, they also must be educated in the resources available assist the officer in preventing them from hurting themselves.

Collectively, agencies need to become part of the solution and no longer the problem. In order for this problem to be managed, it has to be publicly recognized and properly addressed. Leaders should never tolerate false reports designed to make a suicide look like an accident and should accurately report when an officer commits suicide. This problem is easily identified by the inaccuracy of documented suicides when the Federal uniform crime reports are compared to the verified suicides documented by the National Police Suicide Foundation.

Family members should be included in the prevention training to identify officers at risk from changes of behavior at home. This can be accomplished through formal classroom education, web based training, and prevention material mailed to the home. Leaders need to realize that professional and personal matters undoubtedly impact each other. Family members may be the first line of defense in identifying an officer at risk.

Recommendations for future research include conducting a qualitative study on this topic. This can be accomplished by performing a psychological autopsy on an officer who commits suicide and conducting detailed interviews. This study could be expanded by including a broader participant population. This study could be replicated by administering the instrument to a sample of police recruits and measuring a difference in responses later in their career. This would determine if officers become cynical later in their careers.

References

Adcock, R. (2001). Measurement validity: A shared standard for qualitative and quantitative research. *American Political Science Review, 95,* 529-546.

Bass, B. M. (1990). From transactional to transformational leadership: learning to share the vision. *Organizational Dynamics, Winter,* 19-31.

Bass, B. M. (1997). Does the transactional/transformational leadership transcend organizational and motivational boundaries? *Leadership Quarterly, 52*(1), 130-139.

Bennett, W. W., & Hess, K. M. (1996). *Management and supervision in law enforcement* (2nd ed.). New York, NY: West Publishing Company.

Bensimon, E. M. (1989). Transactional, transformational, and trans-vigorational leaders. *Leadership Abstracts, 2*(6), 1-4.

Berkowitz, S. (1996). *Using qualitative and mixed methods approaches.* New York, NY: McGraw-Hill Irwin.

Brookfield, S. D. (1998). Critically reflective practice. *Journal of Continuing Education in Health Profession, 18*(4), 31-38.

Burns, J. M. (1978). *Leadership.* New York, NY: Harper and Row.

Caldero, M. A., & Crank, J. P. (2004). *Police ethics: the corruption of noble cause* (2nd ed.). Cincinnati, OH: Anderson Publishing.

Chan, F. T. (2003). Performance measurement in a supply chain. *International Journal of Advanced Manufacturing Technology, 7*(1), 534-548.

Cooper, D., & Schindler, P. S. (2006). *Business research methods* (9th ed.). New York, NY: McGraw-Hill Irwin.

Couper, D. C., & Lobitz, S. (1991). The customer is always right: Applying vision, leadership and the problem solving method to community oriented policing. *The Police Chief, 5*(1), 16-23.

Creswell, J. (2001). *Research design: qualitative, quantitative and mixed methods.* Thousand Oaks, Ca: Sage.

Denzin, N. K. (1988). *The Research Act: A Theoretical Introduction to Sociological Methods* (3rd ed.). Englewood Cliffs, NJ: Prentice-Hall.

Diekstra, R.F.W., & Kerkhof, A.J.F.M. (1998). Attitudes towards suicide: Development of a Suicide Attitude Questionnaire (SUIATT). Current Issues in Suicidology, 462-476. Berlin: Springer Verlag.

Douglas, R. (2006). Director's Desk. *The Bridge, 9*(2), 1-2.

Douglas, R. (2006). Retrieved October 1, 2006, from National P.O.L.I.C.E Suicide Foundation Web Site: http://www.psf.org/media.htm

Druker, P. F. (1993). *Innovation and Entrepreneurship.* New York, NY: Collins.

Drummond, D. S. (1976). *Police Culture.* Newbury Park, CA: Sage Press.

Elias, J. L., & Merriam, S. B. (1995). *Philosophical foundations of adult education.* Malabar, FL: Krieger Publishing Company.

Festinger, L. (1957). *Theory of cognitive dissonance.* Stanford, CT: Stanford University Press.

Flick, U. (1998). *An Introduction to Qualitative Research.* London: Sage.

Fontana, A., & Frey, J. H. (1994). Interviewing: The art of science. *Handbook of Qualitative Research,* 361-376.

Goleman, D. (1998). What makes a leader? *Harvard Business Review,* 82-91.

Greene, J. R., Alpert, G. P., & Styles, P. (1992). Values and cultures in two american police departments: lessons from king arthur. *Journal of Contemporary Criminal Justice, 8*(3), 183-207.

Greenleaf, R. K. (1977). *Servant leadership: A journey into the nature of legitimate power and greatness.* Mahwah, NJ: Paulist Press.

Guba, E. G. (1990). The alternative paradigm. *The Paradigm Dialog,* 17-27.

Harrison, S. J. (1998). *Police organizational culture: Using ingrained values to build positive improvement.* Retrieved October 21, 2006, from Pennsylvania State University Web Site: http://www.pamij.com/harrison.html

Heiman, M. F. (1977). Suicide among police. *American Journal of Psychiatry, 134*(1), 1286-1290.

Heinsen, D. L., Kinzel, T., & Ramsay, R. (2001). Suicide and law enforcement: Is suicide intervention a necessary part of police training? In (Ed.), *Police Suicide: Vol. 1. Organizational Approaches* (pp. 105-114). Washington, D.C.: FBI.

Hem, E., Berg, A. M., & Ekeberg, O. (2001). Suicide in police-a critical review. *Suicide and Life Threatening Behavior, 31*(2), 224-233.

Hoadley, C. M. (2004). Methodological alignment in design-based research. *Educational Psychologist, 39*(4), 203-212.

Hoshmand, L. T. (2003). Lessons of history and logical analysis ensure progress in psychological science? *Theory and Psychology, 13,* 39-44.

Howe, K. R. (1988). Against the quantitative-qualitative incompatibility thesis or, dogmas die hard. *Educational Researcher, 17,* 10-16.

Johnson, R. B., & Onwuegbuzie, A. J. (2004). Mixed methods research: A research paradigm whose time has come. *Educational Researcher, 33*(7), 14-26.

Johnson, R. B., & Turner, L. A. (2003). Data collection strategies in mixed methods research. *Handbook of Mixed Methods in Social and Behavioral Research,* 297-319.

Kanungo, R. N. (2001). Ethical values of transactional and transformational leaders. *Canadian Journal of Administrative Sciences, 18*(4), 257-265.

King, K. P. (2005). *Bringing transformative learning to life.* Malabar, Fl: Krieger.

Kluckhohn, C. (1949). *Mirror for man.* New York, NY: McGraw-Hill.

Kouzes, J. M., & Posner, B. Z. (2003). *Leadership Practices Inventory: Facilitator's guide* (3rd ed.). San Francisco, CA: Pfeiffer.

Kuhn, T. S. (1962). *The Structure of Scientific Revolutions.* Chicago, IL: University of Chicago Press.

Lester, D. (1992). Suicide in police officers: A survey of nations. *Police Studies, 15*(1), 146-147.

Lewis, M. W., & Grimes, A. J. (1999). Meta-triangulation: Building theory from multiple paradigms. *academy of management, The Academy of Management Review, 24*(4), 672-690.

Loo, R. (2003). A meta-analysis of police suicide rates: findings and issues. *The American Association of Suicidology, 33*(3), 313-325.

Luna-Reyes, L. R., & Anderson, D. L. (2003). Collecting and analyzing qualitative data for system dynamics: Methods and models. *System Dynamics Review, 19*(4), 271-296.

Massey, A., & Walford, G. (1999). Methodological triangulation, or how to get lost without being found out. *Explorations in Methodology, Studies in Educational Ethnography, 2*(1), 183-197.

Maxwell, J. A. (1992). Understanding of validity in qualitative research. *Harvard Educational Review.*

Mertens, D. M. (1998). *Research methods in education and psychology: Integrating diversity with quantitative and qualitative approaches.* Thousand Oaks, CA: Sage.

Mezirow, J. (1990). *Fostering critical reflection in adulthood: A Guide to Transformative and Emancipatory Learning.* San Francisco: Jossey-Bass.

Miles, M. B., & Huberman, A. M. (1994). *Qualitative Data Analysis: A Sourcebook of New Methods* (2nd ed.). Newbury Park, Ca: Sage.

Miles, M. B., & Huberman, A. M. (1994). *Qualitative Data Analysis* (2nd ed.). Thousand Oaks, CA: Sage.

Onwuegbuzie, A. J., & Teddie, C. (2003). A framework for analyzing data in mixed methods research. *Handbook of Mixed Methods in Social and Behavioral Research,* 351-383.

Patterson, K. A. (2003). *Servant leadership: A theoretical model.* Paper presented at the meeting of the Paper Presented at a Servant Leadership Roundtable. Regent University, VA.

Patton, M. Q. (1990). *Qualitative Evaluation and Research Methods* (2nd ed.). Newbury Park, CA: Sage.

Robson, C. (2002). *Real World Research* (2nd ed.). Malden, MA: Blackwell Publishing.

Rouda, R. H., & Kusy, M. E. (1996). Needs Assessment the First Step. *TAPPI Journal, 79*(3), 1-5.

Rowe, R. (2003). Leaders as servants. *New Zealand Management, 50*(1), 24-25.

Rubin, H. J. (1995). *Qualitative Interviewing: The Art of Hearing Data.* Thousand Oaks, CA: Sage.

Satcher, D. (1999). *The Surgeon General's call to action to prevent suicide 1999.* Washington, DC: U.S. Public Health Service.

Schmuckler, E. (2001). There is hope: A training program for suicide awareness and suicide potential. In (Ed.), *Police Suicide: Vol. 1. Organizational Approaches* (pp. 159-164). Washington, DC: FBI.

Sechrest, L., & Sidana, S. (1995). Quantitative and qualitative methods: Is there an alternative? *Evaluation and Program Planning, 18,* 77-87.

Sewell, J. D. (2001). Police suicide: An executive's perspective. In (Ed.), *Police Suicide: Vol. 1. Organizational Approaches* (pp. 165-171). Washington, DC: FBI.

Sosik, J. J., & Megerian, L. E. (1999). Understanding leader emotional intelligence: The role of self-other agreement on transformational leadership perceptions. *Group and Organization Management, 24*(3), 367-90.

Spears, L. C. (1998). *Insights on Leadership: Service, Spirit, and Servant Leadership.* New York, NY: John Wiley & Sons.

Sullivan, E. (2004). Keeping the confidence. *The RCMP Gazette, 63*(3), 1-2.

Taborada, C. G. (2000). leadership, teamwork, and empowerment. *Cost Engineering, 42*(10), 41-44.

Thrasher, R. R. (September 1999). *Developing policy to combat police suicide.* Paper presented at the meeting titles SUICIDE and LAW ENFORCEMENT. Washington, D.C.

Trochin, W. M. (2006). *Types of designs.* Retrieved October 21, 2006, from Cornell University Web Site: http://soicalreseachmethods.net/kb

United States Air Force (2001). *The Air Force suicide prevention program* (AFPAM 44-160). Washington, D.C.: Government Publishing.

United States Army (1988). *Suicide prevention and psychological autopsy* (DOA 600-24). Washington, D.C.: Government Publishing.

Velsor, E. V., & Leslie, J. B. (1991). *Feedback to Managers: A Guide to Evaluating Multi-Rater Feedback Instruments*. Greensboro, NC: Center for Creative Leadership.

Violanti, J. M. (1995). Trends in police suicide. *Psychological Reports, 77*(1), 688-690.

Violanti, J. M. (1996). *Police suicide: Epidemic in blue*. Springfield, IL: Charles C. Thomas.

Violanti, J. M. (1997). Suicide and the police role: A psychosocial model. *Policing: An International Journal of Police Strategy and Management, 20*(4), 698-715.

Weitzer, R., & Tuch, S. (2006). *Race and policing in america: Conflict and reform*. New York, NY: Cambridge University Press.

Winston, B. E. (2005). *Extending patterson's servant leadership model: Coming full circle*. Paper Presented at the Servant Leadership Roundtable. Regent University, VA.

Xuehong, Q. (2002). Research methods. *Chinese Education & Society, 35*(2), 47-54.

APPENDIX A. REQUEST TO UTILIZE SUIATT

E-mail sent to Dr. Kerkhof in the Neherlands:

Dr. Kerkhof,

My name is Orlando Ramos. I am a doctoral student with Capella University in the United States. I am currently in the dissertation phase of my program and am interested in using your instrument to study the perceptions of police officers and suicide. The information gained through your instrument would be instrumental in creating future suicide prevention training. I am a New Jersey State Trooper. I have actively been researching suicide for four years, since the completion of a suicide death of a friend and co-worker. My committee is formed and I have the honor of having Dr. David Lester as a visiting scholar, and well known suicide expert. Upon completion of my research, I am willing to share my findings with you to further validate the use of your instrument.

My contact information is listed below:

Orlando Ramos

E-mail

Respectfully,

Orlando Ramos

APPENDIX B. APPROVAL TO UTILIZE SUIATT

Return E-mail from Dr. Kerkhof:

Van: ▮
Verzonden: Monday, February 05, 2007 8:18 PM
Aan: ▮
Onderwerp: Request to utilize SUIATT for doctoral dissertation in U.S.

Dear Mr. Ramos,

I am happy to know that you are planning to use the SUIATT in your research on attitudes towards suicide a, o among police officers. I gladly permit you to use the Suiatt, given proper reference is given to the developers (Diekstra and Kerkhof). Here are the most relevant references:

Diekstra, R.F.W., & Kerkhof, A.J.F.M. (1988). Attitudes towards suicide: Development of a Suicide Attitude Questionnaire (SUIATT). In H.J. Möller, A. Schmidtke, & R. Welz (Hrsg.), *Current issues of suicidology* (pp. 462-476). Berlin/Heidelberg: Springer Verlag.

Diekstra, R.F.W., & Kerkhof, A.J.F.M. (1989). Attitudes towards suicide: the development of a suicide-attitude-questionnaire (SUIATT). In R.F.W. Diekstra, R. Maris, S. Platt, A. Schmidtke, & G. Sonneck (Eds.), *Advances in Suicidology: Suicide and its Prevention, The role of attitude and imitation* (pp. 91-107). Leiden: Brill.

Please give my best regards to David Lester.

Bye,

Ad Kerkhof
prof. dr. Ad Kerkhof
Department of Clinical Psychology
Vrije Universiteit
Van der Boechorststraat 1
▮
The Netherlands
020-5988777
▮

APPENDIX C. DEMOGRAPHIC DATA

Demographic Data

1. **Age:** ☐20-24 ☐25-29 ☐ 30-34 ☐ 35-39 ☐ 40-44 ☐45-49 ☐50-54 ☐55+

2. **Gender:** ☐Female ☐Male

3. **Highest Education:** ☐High school ☐AA/AS ☐BA/BS ☐MA/MS ☐PHD

4. **Race/Ethnicity:** ☐ American Indian ☐Caucasian ☐African American ☐Latino ☐Asian Other_____

5. **Relationship Status:** ☐Single ☐Married ☐Divorced ☐Widowed ☐Separated ☐Living together

6. **Religious Preference:** ☐Protestant ☐Catholic ☐Jewish ☐Buddhist ☐Hindu ☐Agnostic ☐Atheist ☐Methodist ☐Non denominational Christian ☐Other _____

7. **Years of law enforcement service:** ☐1-5 ☐6-10 ☐11-15 ☐16-20 ☐21-25 ☐25+

8. **Current Assignment:** ☐Patrol ☐Investigations ☐Administration ☐Training ☐Other

9. **Have you had suicide training in the academy?** ☐Yes ☐No

10. **Have you had suicide training during annual in-service?** ☐Yes ☐No

11. **Has your agency had previous officers commit suicide?** ☐Yes ☐No

12. **How many Suicides has your agency had?** _____

13. **Does you agency have a suicide prevention model?** ☐Yes ☐No

14. **Do you have a funeral policy for Officer Suicides?** ☐Yes ☐No

15. **When an officer completes suicide, who is responsible?** _____

16. **Provide a percentage value for amount of responsibility when an officer completes suicide, equal to 100%.**

____Officer ____Job ____Relationship ____Administration ____Training ____Agency

____Other _____

APPENDIX D. RESEARCH INSTRUMENT

Suicide Attitude Questionairre
Diekstra and Kerkhof, 1989
Revised 1993 by Sharon Valente, Ph.D. and
Judith Saunders, R.N., D NSc.

This questionnaire asks about your attitudes and opinions toward self-destructive behavior, including your thoughts about circumstances under which someone might attempt or commit suicide. There are no right or wrong answers; what matters is **your opinion**.

Some questions ask you to identify circumstances under which you think people in general might decide on suicide. Similar questions will ask when you think it probable that someone 'near and dear' to you might decide on suicide. Finally, you will be asked if there are circumstances under which you might decide on suicide.

In the questions that ask about the one who is **most near and dear** to you, we need to know who that person is for you. Please indicate on the line below who that person is by writing just his or her first name and your relationship to that person. For example: "Jim, my husband," "Maria, my sister," or "Andy, my sweetheart/lover."

The person near and dear to me is _____ Please keep this person in mind when answering the questions about "the person who is most near and dear to me."

DIRECTIONS FOR COMPLETING THIS QUESTIONNAIRE

For all the questions you will have up to five alternate responses. Choose the ONE alternative that seems to be the best for you. Please circle the letter indicating your choice. Remember - there are no right or wrong answers.

DEFINITION OF CHOICES:

A = Definitely Yes   **C** = Don't Know/No Opinion   **D** = Probably No
B = Probably Yes   (Maybe/Maybe Not)   **E** = Definitely No

Examples:

1. Tourists come to Hollywood because they love movie stars.   A--B--C--D--E

2. The kind of fruit I like the best is apples.   A--B--C--D--E

1. How do you feel about the fact that people commit suicide?
    1. I don't know
    2. It is a fairly bad thing
    3. It is a bad thing
    4. It is one of the worst things that can happen
    5. It is the worst thing that can happen

2. In your opinion, is suicide inherited?
    1. Always
    2. In most cases
    3. Sometimes
    4. Seldom
    5. Never

For questions #3 - 17...please circle the letter that best represents your opinion.

REMINDER OF CHOICES:
A = Definitely Yes	**C** = Don't Know/No Opinion	**D** = Probably No
B = Probably Yes	(Maybe/Maybe Not)	**E** = Definitely No

How likely is it for people in general to commit suicide under the following circumstances

3.	If they were old and crippled?	A--B--C--D--E
4.	If they suffered from severe and chronic pain?	A--B--C--D--E
5.	If their partner left them?	A--B--C--D--E
6.	If they became severely disabled?	A--B--C--D--E
7.	If they became unemployed?	A--B--C--D--E
8.	If they had a severely handicapped child?	A--B--C--D--E
9.	If they were admitted to a mental hospital?	A--B--C--D--E
10.	If it were impossible for them to have children?	A--B--C--D--E
11.	If they suffer from an incurable illness?	A--B--C--D--E
12.	If they suffer from a terminal illness?	A--B--C--D--E
13.	If the person(s) most near and dear to them dies?	A--B--C--D--E
14.	If they have Alzheimer's disease?	A--B--C--D--E

15. If they do not succeed in finding a life partner?   A--B--C--D--E

16. If they have killed someone else?   A--B--C--D--E

17. If they have AIDS?   A--B--C--D--E

18. In your opinion, do people commit suicide because they are mentally ill?
    1. Always
    2. Most of the time
    3. Sometimes
    4. Seldom
    5. Never

19. Do you believe that one has the right to commit suicide?
    1. Always
    2. Most of the time
    3. Sometimes
    4. Seldom
    5. Never

20. If people commit suicide, the consequences for society as a whole are:
    1. Always negative
    2. Often negative
    3. Sometimes negative/Sometimes positive
    4. Often positive
    5. Always positive

Reminder of Choices:
A = Definitely Yes   C = Don't Know/No Opinion   D = Probably No
B = Probably Yes   (Maybe/Maybe Not)   E = Definitely No

Do you think that someone who makes a suicide attempt:

21. Intends to force or manipulate things in his/her way?   A--B--C--D--E

22. Intended to point out to others how big his/her problems are?   A--B--C--D--E

23. Intends to die?   A--B--C--D--E

24. Is mentally ill?   A--B--C--D--E

25. Write in any other reason you personally would also take into consideration. If none, please write NONE _____

26. How likely do you think it is that you will end your life by suicide?
    1. Very unlikely
    2. Fairly unlikely
    3. Don't know
    4. Fairly likely
    5. Very likely

27. If you were to commit suicide, would you find this --
    1. Very cowardly
    2. Fairly cowardly
    3. Somewhat cowardly
    4. Only a little cowardly
    5. Not cowardly at all

28. If you were to commit suicide, would you find this --
    1. Very brave
    2. Fairly brave
    3. Somewhat brave
    4. Only a little brave
    5. Not brave at all

29. If the person most near and dear to you would commit suicide, how would you feel about that?
    1. That would be the worst thing that could happen to me
    2. That would be one of the worst things that could happen to me
    3. That would be a bad thing for me
    4. I don't know how I would feel about that
    5. That would not be a bad thing for me

30. Do you believe that if someone commits suicide,
    1. It is a very deliberate act
    2. It probably is a deliberate act
    3. Don't know
    4. It probably is an impulsive act
    5. It is a very impulsive act

31. Would you be willing to help prevent self-destructive behavior of suicidal persons by talking with or contacting them?
    1. Certainly
    2. Probably
    3. Don't know
    4. Probably not
    5. certainly not

32. When someone commits suicide, the consequences of this act for those closest to him/her are:
　　1. Always negative
　　2. Often negative
　　3. Perhaps negative/perhaps positive
　　4. Often positive
　　5. Always positive

33. Do you think that in order to commit suicide, you have to be mentally ill?
　　1. Definitely yes
　　2. Probably yes
　　3. Maybe/maybe not
　　4. Probably no
　　5. Definitely no

REMINDER OF CHOICES:
　　A=Definitely Yes　　**C**=Don't Know/No Opinion　　**D**=Probably No
　　B=Probably Yes　　　　(Maybe/Maybe Not)　　　　　　**E**=Definitely No

If the **person most near and dear to you** makes a suicide attempt, he or she:

34. Intends to force or manipulate things his/her own way.　　A--B--C--D--E

35. Intends to point out how big his/her problems are.　　　　A--B--C--D--E

36. Intends to die.　　　　　　　　　　　　　　　　　　　　A--B--C--D--E

37. Is mentally ill.　　　　　　　　　　　　　　　　　　　　A--B--C--D--E

38. Write in any other reason you would take into consideration. If none, please write NONE. _____

39. If the person most near and dear to you were to commit suicide, would you object to newspapers reporting it?
　　1. Definitely Yes
　　2. Probably Yes
　　3. Don't Know
　　4. Probably No
　　5. Definitely No

REMINDER OF CHOICES:
  A=Definitely Yes   C=Don't Know/No Opinion   D=Probably No
  B=Probably Yes   (Maybe/Maybe Not)   E=Definitely No

How likely do you think it would be for the **person most near and dear to you** to commit suicide under the following circumstances:

40. If she/he were old and crippled? A--B--C--D--E

41. If she/he suffered from severe and chronic pain? A--B--C--D--E

42. If her/his partner left? A--B--C--D--E

43. If she/he were severely disabled? A--B--C--D--E

44. If she/he had AIDS? A--B--C--D--E

45. If she/he were unemployed? A--B--C--D--E

46. If she/he were to have (had) a severely handicapped child? A--B--C--D--E

47. If she/he were taken to a mental hospital? A--B--C--D--E

48. If it were impossible for her/him to have children? A--B--C--D--E

49. If she/he were to suffer from a incurable illness? A--B--C--D--E

50. If she/he were to suffer from a terminal illness? A--B--C--D--E

51. If she/he were to become bereaved of the person(s) most near and dear? A--B--C--D--E

52. If she/he did not succeed in finding a partner for life? A--B--C--D--E

53. If she/he had killed someone else? A--B--C--D--E

54. If she/he had Alzheimer's disease? A--B--C--D--E

55. Please write in your opinion of another circumstance that might apply:
_____

Do you think for him/her there would be a likelihood of suicide under the circumstance that you have noted above? A--B--C--D--E

REMINDER OF CHOICES:

    A=Definitely Yes   C=Don't know/No opinion   D=Probably No
    B=Probably Yes   (Maybe/Maybe Not)   E=Definitely No

Under what circumstance might you commit suicide?

56. If you were old and crippled?   A--B--C--D--E

57. If you suffered from severe and chronic pain?   A--B--C--D--E

58. If your partner left you?   A--B--C--D--E

59. If you had AIDS?   A--B--C--D--E

60. If you became severely disabled?   A--B--C--D--E

61. If you became unemployed?   A--B--C--D--E

62. If you had a severely handicapped child?   A--B--C--D--E

63. If you were admitted to a mental hospital?   A--B--C--D--E

64. If it were impossible for you to have children?   A--B--C--D--E

65. If you suffered from an incurable illness?   A--B--C--D--E

66. If you suffered from a terminal illness?   A--B--C--D--E

67. If the person (s) most near and dear to you dies?   A--B--C--D--E

68. If you do not succeed in finding a life partner?   A--B--C--D--E

69. If you had killed someone else?   A--B--C--D--E

70. If you had Alzheimer's Disease?   A--B--C--D--E

71. Write in any other reason you think might cause you to commit suicide. If none, please write none. _____

72. How do you feel about putting an end to your own life?
    1. That would be the worst thing I could do
    2. That would be one of the worst things I could do
    3. That would be a bad thing for me to do
    4. That would not be a bad thing for me to do
    5. Don't know/No opinion

73. Thanks for continuing !

74. Indicate which way of dying you would prefer for <u>yourself</u>. Put one number (1,2,3,4) for each cause.

   1 = least preferred
   2 = next least preferred
   3 = next most preferred
   4 = most preferred

   _____Murder
   _____Natural causes (illness, old age)
   _____Accident
   _____Suicide

75. Do you believe that in <u>your ideal society</u>, suicide would
   1. Certainly not occur
   2. Probably not occur
   3. Don't know/No opinion
   4. Probably occur
   5. Certainly occur

76. Do you believe in <u>your current society</u>, suicide would
   1. Certainly not occur.
   2. Probably not occur.
   3. Don't know/No opinion
   4. Probably occur.
   5. Certainly occur.

77. What is your opinion about suicide prevention efforts in the United States?
   1. Very negative
   2. Fairly negative
   3. Don't know/No opinion
   4. Fairly positive
   5. Very positive

78. If you were to commit suicide, would you object to newspapers reporting it?
   1. Definitely yes
   2. Probably yes
   3. Don't know
   4. Probably no
   5. Definitely no

79. The death of the person most near and dear to you would undoubtedly be distressing for you. Nevertheless, the way he or she might die could influence how you would feel about it. Please rank the following possible causes of death of the <u>person most near and dear to you</u> by putting the number (1,2,3,4) preceding the listed cause.

    1= Most disrupting or upsetting cause of death.
    2= the next most disrupting cause of death.
    3= the next least disrupting cause of death.
    4= the least disrupting cause of death.

    _____ Murder
    _____ Natural (illness/old age)
    _____ Suicide
    _____ Accident

80. If the <u>person most near and dear to you</u> were to tell you that he/she wants to commit suicide, would you take this communication:
    1. Very seriously
    2. Rather seriously
    3. Probably not very seriously
    4. Not seriously
    5. No opinion/Don't know

81. If <u>you</u> were to commit suicide, it would:
    1. Be a very deliberate act
    2. Probably be a deliberate act
    3. Probably be an impulsive act
    4. Be a very impulsive act
    5. No opinion/Don't know

82. Have you ever attempted suicide?
    1. Very often (7 or more times)
    2. Often (4-6 times)
    3. More than once (2-3 times)
    4. Once
    5. Never

83. If <u>you</u> were to commit suicide, the consequences of this act for those closest to you are:
    1. Always negative
    2. Often negative
    3. Sometimes negative/sometimes positive
    4. Often positive
    5. Always positive

84. When someone commits suicide, do you object to newspapers reporting it?
    1. Definitely yes
    2. Probably yes
    3. No opinion/Don't know
    4. Probably no
    5. Definitely no

85. If the person most near and dear to you were to commit suicide. It would:
    1. Be a very deliberate act
    2. Probably be a deliberate act
    3. No opinion/don't know
    4. Probably be an impulsive act
    5. Be a very impulsive act

86. If the person most near and dear to you were to commit suicide, would you find this:
    1. Very cowardly
    2. Fairly cowardly
    3. No opinion
    4. Probably not cowardly
    5. Definitely not cowardly

87. If the person most near and dear to you were to commit suicide, would you find this:
    1. Very brave
    2. Fairly brave
    3. No opinion
    4. Probably not brave
    5. Definitely not brave

88. When someone attempts suicide, the consequences of this act for his or herself are:
    1. Always negative
    2. Often negative
    3. Perhaps negative/perhaps positive
    4. Often positive
    5. Always positive

89. If you were to commit suicide, what method would you most probably use?
    1. Hanging
    2. Drowning
    3. Gas
    4. Pills/Poison
    5. Stabbing
    6. Jumping from a height
    7. Jumping in front of a car
    8. Guns
    9. Other: _____

REMINDER OF CHOICES:
    A=Definitely Yes   C=Don't Know/No Opinion   D=Probably No
    B=Probably Yes   (Maybe/Maybe Not)   E=Definitely No

90. If someone asked you to assist with his/her suicide, would you be willing to do so?   A--B--C--D--E

91. If someone were planning to commit suicide, would you be willing to prevent the act?   A--B--C--D--E

92. If the person most near and dear to you were ask you to to assist with his/her suicide, would you be willing to do so?   A--B--C--D--E

93. If the person most near and dear to you were to plan to commit suicide, would you be willing to prevent the suicide?   A--B--C--D--E

94. Do you believe you have the right to commit suicide?
    1. Always
    2. Most of the time
    3. Don't know/No opinion
    4. Sometimes
    5. Never

APPENDIX E. LETTER OF REQUEST

April 1, 2007

Robert E. Douglas Jr.
Executive Director
National Police Suicide Foundation

Dear: Director Douglas

Subject: PROPOSED RESEARCH

As you know, I am employed as a Trooper with the New Jersey State Police. I am also a full-time student at Capella University and am working toward my PhD in Organization and Management. As a part of my final degree requirements, I will be completing my dissertation in the area of leadership and training with respect to police suicide. Specifically, I will be identifying factors that are associated with positive and negative attitudes towards suicide. The title of my research is "Police Suicide Perceptions: Providing Leaders an Understanding to a Complicated Problem as Measured Through the Suicide Attitude Questionnaire (SUIATT)." I am hoping this research contributes to the law enforcement community and is beneficial to law enforcement executives.

As per our telephone conversation, I am requesting to use the data you recently collected from the SUIATT instrument. I intend to compare and contrast the information between two groups, east coast officers and west coast officers. I will also examine the data separately to determine if there is a correlation between demographic data and suicide perceptions. I believe this information would be helpful for supervisors to develop future training and to identify additional risk factors among their members. It is my understanding that there is no identifiable personal information on these surveys. I request that any attendance rosters be omitted from the group of surveys to ensure anonymity of participants. I will assume any costs related to shipping and handling of the instruments.

Capella University Human Subjects Institutional Review Board (IRB) will review and approve my research proposal. A copy of the IRB approval will be made available to you prior to data collection. You may contact me directly with any questions or concerns at ▮▮▮▮▮. You may also contact my committee chair, Dr. Kathleen Henry at ▮▮▮▮▮. Capella requires a written response on official letter head to be submitted with the IRB application. This can be forwarded directly to my home address, which you have on file. Thank you for your contribution to the field of police suicide and your assistance in this research.

Respectfully,

Orlando Ramos
Doctoral Candidate
Capella University
School of Business
225 South 6th Street, 9th Floor
Minneapolis, Minnesota 55402

APPENDIX F. LETTER OF PERMISSION

THE NATIONAL P.O.L.I.C.E. SUICIDE FOUNDATION, INC.
8424 Park Road
Pasadena, Maryland 21122

Dr. Kathleen Henry
Capilla University
Institutional Review Board (IRB)

Re: Release of Suicide Attitude Questionnaire (SUIATT)

Dear Dr. Henry,

As Executive Director of the National P.O.L.I.C.E. Suicide Foundation, Inc., I hereby release all Suicide Attitude Questionnaires (SUIATT) that have been collected for Doctoral Candidate Orlando Ramos in his titled research "Police Suicide Prospective".

If you have any further requests, please do not hesitate to contact me.

Respectfully,

Robert E. Douglas Jr.
Executive Director

Phone: (410) 437-3343   Fax: (410) 437-3343   Redoug2001@aol.com

DOWNTOWN CAMPUS LRC

J.S. Reynolds Community College
3 7219 00171135 0

HV 7936 .S77 R366 2008
Ramos, Orlando.
A leadership perspective for understanding police

CPSIA information can be obtained at www.ICGtesting.com
Printed in the USA
LVOW111607040313
322627LV00008B/375/A

9 781581 123876